PARTS Ist ENGLISH Part Viz ENGLISH EMPIRE containing ye Articklands near Hudsons Bay New North
na Carolania or Florida California, Sommer Ie Bahama Ie Jamaica &c CARIBY Ie II S'PANISH
ARCTICK LAND
BAFF BAY
NEW NORTH WALES
NEW SOUTH WALES
HUDSONS BAY
Hudsons Straits
TERRA LABRADOR
NEW BRITAIN
NEW FOUND LAND
The Main Bank
False Bank
L. PISCOUTAGAMI
L. TABITIBIS
NEW FRANCE
LAKE SUPERIOR
LAKE HURONS
LAKE ILINOIS
LAKE ERIE
Cape Cod
SEA OF THE ENGLISH EMPIRE
Bermudes als Summer Ilands
Tract of Land of Wild Bulls
THE GOLF OR BAY OF MEXICO
BAHAMA ISLANDS
ANTILLES Ie
WEST INDIAN SEA
CARIBY ISLANDS
JAMAICA
YUCATAN
HONDURAS
ANDALUSIA
PARIA
Barbados
C. Florida
AIN

•VOICES• *from* COLONIAL AMERICA

VIRGINIA

1607–1776

SANDRA POBST

WITH

KEVIN D. ROBERTS, PH.D., CONSULTANT

NATIONAL GEOGRAPHIC

WASHINGTON, D.C.

One of the world's largest nonprofit scientific and educational organizations, the National Geographic Society was founded in 1888 "for the increase and diffusion of geographic knowledge." Fulfilling this mission, the Society educates and inspires millions every day through its magazine, books, television programs, videos, maps and atlases, research grants, the National Geographic Bee, teacher workshops, and innovative classroom materials. The Society is supported through membership dues, charitable gifts, and income from the sale of its educational products. This support is vital to National Geographic's mission to increase global understanding and promote conservation of our planet through exploration, research, and education.

For more information, please call 1-800-NGS LINE (647-5463) or write to the following address:

NATIONAL GEOGRAPHIC SOCIETY
1145 17th Street N.W.
Washington, D.C. 20036-4688
U.S.A.

Visit the Society's Web site at www.nationalgeographic.com.

STAFF FOR THIS BOOK

Nancy Laties Feresten, *Vice President, Editor-in-Chief of Children's Books*
Suzanne Patrick Fonda, *Project Editor*
Robert D. Johnston, Ph.D., *Associate Professor and Director, Teaching of History Program University of Illinois at Chicago, Overall Series Editor*
Bea Jackson, *Design Director, Children's Books and Education Publishing Group*
Jean Cantu, *Illustrations Specialist*
Carl Mehler, *Director of Maps*
Justin Morrill, *The M Factory, Inc., Map Research, Design, and Production*
Connie D. Binder, *Indexer*
Rebecca Hinds, *Managing Editor*
R. Gary Colbert, *Production Director*
Lewis R. Bassford, *Production Manager*
Vincent P. Ryan and Maryclare Tracy, *Manufacturing Managers*

Voices from Colonial Virginia was prepared by CREATIVE MEDIA APPLICATIONS, INC.

Sandra Pobst, *Writer*
Fabia Wargin Design, Inc., *Design and Production*
Matt Levine, *Editor*
Susan Madoff, *Associate Editor*
Laurie Lieb, *Copyeditor*
Jennifer Bright, *Image Researcher*

Body text is set in Deepdene, sidebars are Caslon 337 Oldstyle, and display text is Cochin Archaic Bold.

LIBRARY OF CONGRESS CATALOGING-IN-PUBLICATION DATA

Pobst, Sandy.
Virginia, 1607–1776 / by Sandy Pobst.
p. cm. — (Voices from colonial America)
Includes bibliographical references and index.
ISBN 0-7922-6388-X (Hardcover)
ISBN 0-7922-6771-0 (Library)
1. Virginia—History—Colonial period, ca. 1600–1775—Juvenile literature. I. Title. II. Series.
F229.P783 2005
975.5'02—dc22

2005008885

Printed in Belgium

Contents

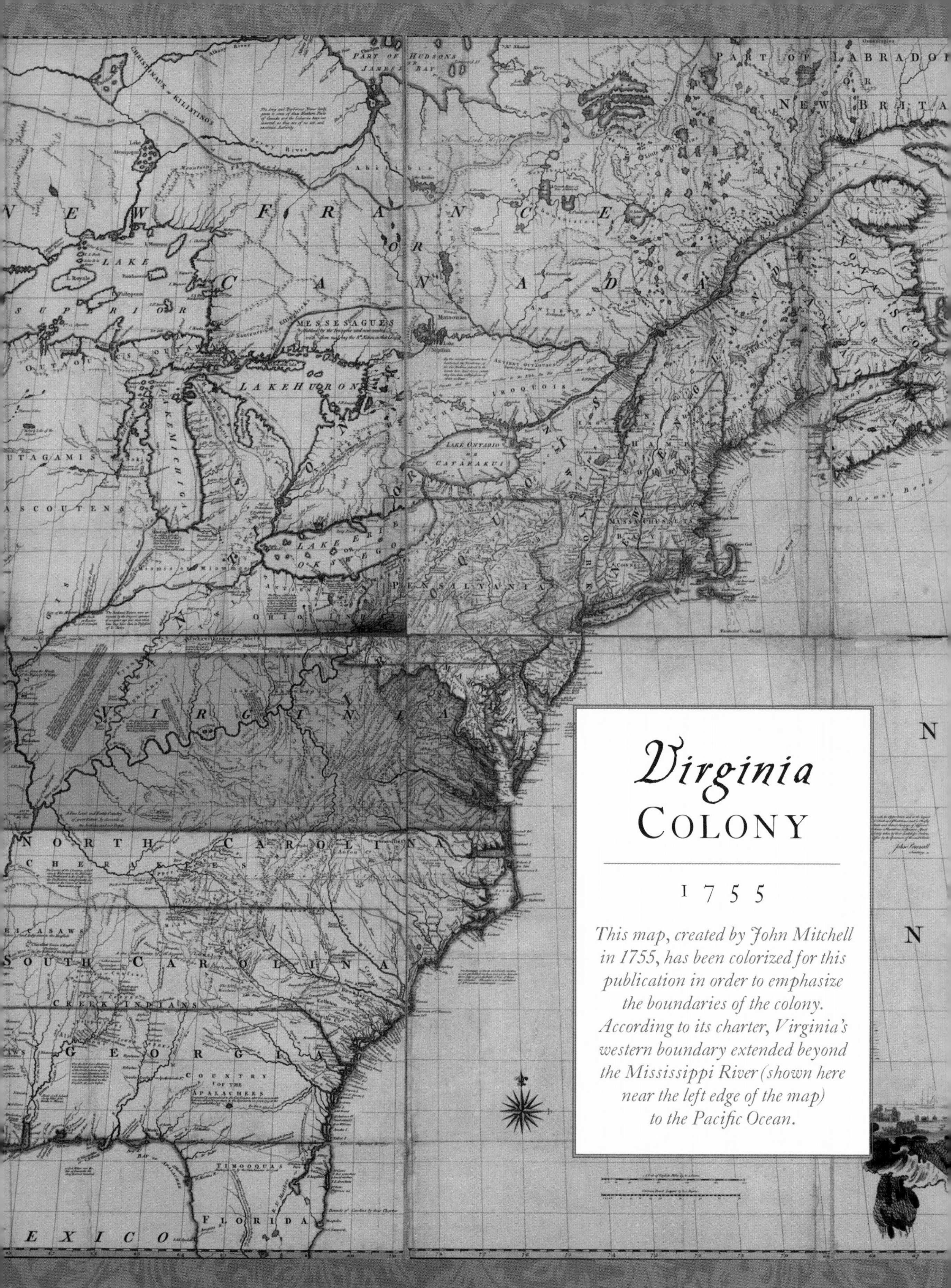

Virginia COLONY

1755

This map, created by John Mitchell in 1755, has been colorized for this publication in order to emphasize the boundaries of the colony. According to its charter, Virginia's western boundary extended beyond the Mississippi River (shown here near the left edge of the map) to the Pacific Ocean.

INTRODUCTION

by

Kevin D. Roberts, Ph.D.

The Jamestown settlement in Virginia, pictured here in 1607 in a colored engraving, was the first permanent English settlement in the New World.

The story of the United States begins in Virginia. It was here on a malaria-infested peninsula in the James River that the first permanent English settlement in the New World was founded nearly 400 years ago.

Lured by the promise of finding gold, the "planters," as the daring settlers were called, set sail full of confidence. Some had money of their own to pay for the voyage. Others gained free passage by agreeing to work for a number of years in the colony. None were prepared for the hardships that would bring suffering and death at Jamestown—drought, disease, Indian attacks, and starvation. The threat of abandonment by the investors who had financed the colony made them more determined than ever to succeed. New leadership brought some improvement, but it was the "devil's weed" that saved the colony from destruction.

In 1613 John Rolfe sent the first shipment of his Virginia-grown West Indian tobacco to England where it was an instant success. By mid-century the demand for tobacco had become so great that the plant became known as "green gold."

The crop that saved Virginia also became its curse. The prosperity it brought created a bitter rivalry between wealthy Tidewater plantation owners and freed servants who had become farmers on the western frontier. In 1676 these tensions erupted in a civil war known as Bacon's Rebellion. Although short lived, the rebellion had a lasting effect on Virginia society. Fearful of future revolts, plantation owners began replacing white laborers with African slaves. By 1750 slave labor had made the colony the wealthiest in British America.

By the time of the American Revolution, Virginia had come full circle from a backwater, dependent colony to one of the most successful in North America. Ironically, some of the men who profited most from the colony's slave-based economy were among the leading supporters of America's right to be free from British rule and would play key roles in the war for independence.

The Seal of the Virginia Colony appeared on official documents and was often painted on government buildings. The seal can still be seen today on the tower of the Colonial Capitol Building in Williamsburg, Virginia.

I am delighted to serve as the historical consultant for *Voices from Colonial America: Virginia*. I often ask my students to imagine that they are a particular person from the past—say a plantation owner, a slave, Native American, or soldier, just to name a few possibilities from colonial Virginia. This allows them to step away from their high-tech lifestyles into the world of people who braved the challenges of a new land. Think of this book as your road map to understanding the lives of those early colonists and how they helped form the history of Virginia and the United States.

CHAPTER ONE

Establishing a Colony

AMBITIOUS ENGLISHMEN *expect to get rich by establishing a colony in North America but soon find out that colonization is harder than they think.*

In 1558, the country of England faced several problems. A rapidly growing population was placing severe strains on the nation's resources. Religious conflicts were causing tension between Roman Catholics and Protestants. Finally, Spain was quickly becoming the most powerful country in Europe—a situation that made England's citizens very nervous.

Some of England's most ambitious men were gentlemen from the southwest part of the country who had connections

OPPOSITE: In 1584, men sent by Sir Walter Ralegh landed on a barrier island off the coast of present-day North Carolina. They claimed the land for England according to the charter granted by the Queen.

at court. Known as the "West Country men," they introduced bold ideas to increase England's power. One such plan was to establish English colonies in the New World.

English colonies along the mid- and north Atlantic coast of North America would provide several advantages. First, colonies might be a source of gold, silver, and other natural resources that would make England (and themselves) richer. This wealth could be used to strengthen the British Navy and help prevent a takeover by Spain. The location would also provide an opportunity for privateers. They could carry supplies from England to the colony, unload their cargo, and then sail to the Caribbean to try to capture Spanish treasure ships. (The colony of New Spain was a source of gold.) Finally, thousands of unemployed men and women could be sent to the colonies, providing a steady source of cheap labor in the New World and making cities in England safer.

colony—a settlement that is controlled by a distant country

privateer—a sailor who has the government's permission to capture foreign ships

England's Queen Elizabeth supported the idea of establishing colonies in North America. With little money in the royal treasury, however, England could not afford such a venture. Instead, Elizabeth encouraged individuals to support the cost of colonization. In return, these individuals received charters promising them ownership of any land they colonized.

charter—a written document that granted its holder (either an individual or a company) the right to colonize and own land in a foreign country

In 1578, Sir Humphrey Gilbert received a charter to establish the first English colony in the New World. Gilbert, a former military commander, raised the money for the new colony from wealthy investors. Each investor was promised ownership of land in the colony. The actual work of clearing the land, planting crops, building houses, and so forth would be done by English settlers and Native Americans. Earlier English explorers had reported their encounters with Indians living along the eastern coast of North America. Gilbert and others believed that the Indians would work for the colonists willingly once the Indians saw the comforts that English civilization offered.

In 1583, Gilbert claimed Newfoundland in present-day Canada for England, intending to found a colony there. However, Gilbert's ship was lost at sea on the voyage home. The colony was never established.

Ralegh* Steps Up

When Gilbert's charter expired in 1584, Queen Elizabeth awarded it to Sir Walter Ralegh. Ralegh was one of Queen Elizabeth's favorite courtiers. The charter granted ownership of any land in North America on which Ralegh could establish a colony. He could also claim all the land 600 miles (965 km) to the north and south of the colony, as long as it wasn't inhabited or

courtier—an attendant at a royal court

**This spelling reflects the latest scholarly thinking on how Ralegh actually spelled his name.*

claimed by people from a Christian nation. (During this time period, "Christian" was often used to describe European, or white, people and excluded Native Americans.) A western border wasn't specified, since no one knew how far west the continent extended.

Ralegh wasted no time in arranging an expedition to locate a site for his colony. Unwilling to chance Ralegh being lost at sea, Queen Elizabeth wouldn't allow him to go on the expedition. Instead, Arthur Barlowe and Philip Amadas, associates of Ralegh, led the voyage.

On April 27, 1584, Barlowe and Amadas set sail for North America. By mid-July, the two small ships had anchored near Hatorasck Island (now known as Hatteras Island) off the coast of present-day North Carolina. The men claimed the island, along with the rest of the Atlantic coast from what is now Canada to Spanish Florida, for Queen Elizabeth and England.

Over the next few days, the men discovered they were on a barrier island. In his report to Ralegh, Barlowe wrote, "*This Island had many goodly woods full of Deer, Conies [rabbits], Hares, and Fowl.*" He also noted that between the barrier island and the mainland were "*above a hundreth Islands of divers bignesses . . . replenished with goodly Cedars, and divers other sweet woods, full of Currants [a kind of berry], of flax, and many other notable commodities.*"

barrier island—a narrow island that lies parallel to the mainland and protects it from being battered by ocean waves

flax—a plant with soft fibers that can be made into cloth

commodity—anything that can be bought, sold, or traded

PROFILE

Sir Walter Ralegh

Sir Walter Ralegh was born in southwestern England around 1554. Ralegh left home when he was 15. He fought in foreign wars, sailed in search of new lands, and helped crush the 1580 rebellion in Ireland. Ralegh's successes gained him an introduction at court. There, Queen Elizabeth helped him become wealthy and powerful.

When Elizabeth died, her cousin James I became king. Ralegh's enemies convinced the new king that Ralegh had plotted against him. James sentenced Ralegh to death, but later changed the punishment to life in prison. In 1616, Ralegh convinced the king to let him sail to South America to search for gold. When Ralegh attacked the Spanish there against his king's wishes, James reinstated Ralegh's death sentence. After Ralegh was beheaded in 1618, his wife embalmed his head, keeping it until her death 29 years later. (The head was then buried with Ralegh in London, England.)

Sir Walter Ralegh is pictured with his son in a painting from 1602.

Meeting the Roanoke Indians

Four days after the English landed, a group of Roanoke Indians arrived on Hatorasck Island. After several days of trading, Barlowe and seven other Europeans traveled to Roanoke Island to visit the Indians' village. Barlowe described the native inhabitants as *"very handsome and goodly people, and in their behavior as mannerly and civil as any in Europe."* Later, Barlowe wrote, *"We found the people most gentle, loving, and faithful."*

This colored engraving by Theodore de Bry illustrates an elder from one of the Indian tribes that the English colonists encountered upon landing at Roanoke Island.

Soon afterward, Barlowe and Amadas sailed back to England. Manteo and Wanchese, two Indians of the Croatoan and Roanoke tribes, traveled with them. The explorers also carried a sack of pearls they had received in trade as an example of the natural resources available in the new land.

Roanoke Colony

Barlowe's report excited Ralegh, who proposed naming the rich land Virginia, in honor of Queen Elizabeth. (Elizabeth was known as the Virgin Queen because she had never married.) Elizabeth knighted Ralegh as a reward for the success of the voyage. Ralegh began promoting his plans to establish a permanent colony in Virginia. He also recruited colonists to make the journey to America.

On April 9, 1585, Ralegh bid farewell to the 108 colonists

The First Americans *in England*

Few details are known about Manteo's and Wanchese's experiences in England. They apparently traveled willingly to England with the explorers. Ralegh introduced the pair at court and used them to promote his colony.

During their six-month stay in England, Manteo and Wanchese learned to speak some English. Thomas Hariot, who would later travel to Virginia with the first group of colonists, spent a great deal of time with the two Indians. They taught him some of their language and shared information about their culture.

Upon their return to Virginia in July 1585, Manteo stayed with the colonists, serving as a translator and guide. Wanchese, however, grew increasingly frustrated with the arrogance of the English settlers. He would later lead attacks against the colonists.

bound for Virginia. The fleet reached Roanoke Island in July—too late to plant crops such as wheat or corn that could be harvested before winter. To complicate matters, the ship carrying the supplies ran aground, and what little food was on board was ruined. The naval commander—Sir Richard Grenville—promised to bring more supplies when he returned in the spring.

Ralegh had appointed Ralph Lane to serve as governor of the colony. All of the colonists who accompanied Lane were men. There were several gentlemen who were not used to hard work or rough surroundings. Other colonists were skilled laborers, while some were soldiers. None of them was accustomed to growing his own food. They were not skilled hunters, and they had no idea which foods to gather to eat. Instead, the Englishmen relied upon the Indians to provide food.

The settlers built an earthen fort on the north end of Roanoke Island. Known as Fort Ralegh, the structure stretched about 50 feet (15 m) on each side. The men built houses outside the walls of the fort. Letters and reports from Lane and other colonists describe the houses as cottages that stood one and a half to two stories high, with thatched roofs. Pieces of brick and brick-making equipment that have been found at the site of the fort indicate that the houses may have had brick foundations and chimneys.

Once the fort was built, a group of colonists set off to explore the region. Among them were Thomas Hariot, a scientist and mathematician, and John White, an artist. Hariot later published a book, *A Briefe and True Report of the New Found Land of Virginia,* which described the plant and animal life they found. Engravings made from White's sketches and paintings were included in the book. Much of what is known today about the Indian tribes who lived along the mid-Atlantic coast in the 16th century comes from Hariot's and White's observations.

When John White arrived in Virginia in 1585, he painted numerous watercolors. This 1590 colored engraving by Theodore de Bry is based on White's work. The map shows European ships approaching the string of barrier islands that protects the Atlantic coast along what is now North Carolina. Readers should note that the map is drawn with the North at the right edge of the map, rather than the top edge.

Virginia's Native People

A 1590 colored engraving by Theodore de Bry is based on John White's watercolor of a Roanoke Indian village. Longhouses, the tunnel-shaped homes favored by the Roanoke, were placed throughout the well-ordered village.

The Roanoke Indians were members of the Roanoke, or Secotan, Nation. Their leader was Wingina. His empire stretched as far south and west as the Neuse River in present-day North Carolina. The Roanoke Indians—like the Croatoan and other nearby tribes—were part of the larger Algonquian family of tribes.

The Roanoke lived in small villages. Each family in a village had its own longhouse, a tunnel-shaped house covered with mats made of reed or bark. The werowance lived in the largest house, which was usually built opposite the temple.

werowance—an Algonquian chief

Men hunted deer, turkeys, and other game using bows and arrows. They also fished, using spears, nets, and traps called weirs. Women raised corn, squash, beans, and tobacco in village fields. In the spring and summer, women gathered wild berries and other fruits. In the winter, the entire village moved westward to hunt for deer.

Troubled Times

The colonists relied heavily on the Indians for food that winter. By spring, the Roanoke were tired of the colonists' demands for food. They refused to share what little they had left. The colonists were soon on the verge of starvation.

Governor Lane became convinced that Wingina—now known as Pemisapan—was plotting to attack the colonists, so Lane attacked Pemisapan's village on June 1, 1586. When the battle ended, Pemisapan was dead. The Roanoke, who had once welcomed the English, were now their bitter enemies.

Relief Arrives

Starving and desperate, the colonists moved to Hatorasck and the other barrier islands. There, they lived on oysters. On June 9, 1586, one group spotted an English fleet approaching.

Sir Francis Drake, a privateer, commanded the fleet. He offered Lane a ship and a month's worth of supplies if the colonists wanted to stay. In the end, however, Lane decided that all the colonists would return to England with Drake.

Two weeks later, Grenville arrived. He had sailed to the Caribbean before going to England to get supplies and had taken almost a year to return. He left 15 men and supplies at the abandoned Fort Ralegh, and set sail for England.

The Lost Colony

Ralegh would not give up. In May 1587, 117 colonists boarded three ships financed by Ralegh. The men, known as "planters," were each promised at least 500 acres (200 ha) of land. This time, some of the planters took their wives and children with them. Ralegh selected John White, the artist from the first expedition, as the governor.

Ralegh directed the colonists to establish a fort near Chesapeake Bay. Instead, the colonists landed at Roanoke Island in July 1587. There, they found Grenville's men missing, the fort torn down, and the houses abandoned. The colonists decided to stay at Roanoke. However, it was too late in the year to plant crops. The expedition had once again failed to bring enough food for the winter, and the settlers could get no help from the Native Americans.

On August 18, 1587, the colonists celebrated the birth of Virginia Dare—the first English child born in America and the granddaughter of Governor White. Soon afterward, White returned to England for supplies. Just after he reached England, war broke out with Spain. All ships were placed under control of the British Navy. Three years passed before White could return to America.

When White arrived with a relief ship in August 1590, the houses had been long abandoned. Carved into a post was the word "CROATOAN." White thought the carvings meant that the colonists had traveled to Croatoan

Island (site of present-day Ocracoke Island) to stay with the friendly Croatoan Indians.

Although White sailed for Croatoan Island, a hurricane turned his ship out into the Atlantic and forced him to head back to England. White was never able to finance another trip to Virginia to search for his family and the other colonists.

No one ever found out what happened to the colonists left by John White in 1587. Some believe that the group split into smaller bands that resettled throughout the region.

The most recent theory about what has become known as the Lost Colony indicates that between 1587 and 1590, Roanoke Island and the surrounding area experienced the most severe drought in more than 800 years. With little rain to nourish crops, the colonists may have been forced to move to another area.

In the early 1700s, English explorer John Lawson spent time with the descendants of the Croatoan tribe on Hatteras Island. He reported the Indians' claim that *"several of their Ancestors were white People . . . the Truth of which is confirm'd by gray Eyes being found frequently amongst these Indians, and no others."*

In the 1880s, hunters came across a group of Indians living in present-day North Carolina. These Indians had fair hair and blue or gray eyes and claimed their ancestors were from "Roanoke in Virginia." Their English was similar to that spoken in 16th-century England, and many had the same last names as settlers from the Lost Colony.

NOVA BRITANNIA.

OFFERING MOST

Excellent fruites by Planting in

VIRGINIA.

Exciting all ſuch as be well affected
to further the ſame.

LONDON
Printed for SAMVEL MACHAM, and are to beſold at
his Shop in Pauls Church-yard, at the
Signe of the Bul-head.
1609.

Trying Again

CULTURES COLLIDE *when English colonists settle on land ruled by the powerful Powhatan Confederacy.*

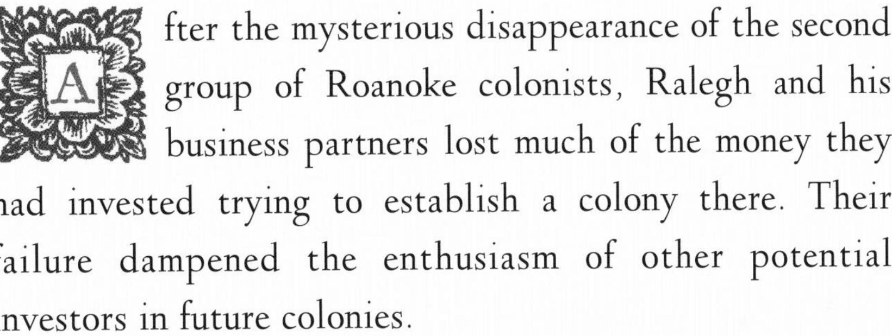

After the mysterious disappearance of the second group of Roanoke colonists, Ralegh and his business partners lost much of the money they had invested trying to establish a colony there. Their failure dampened the enthusiasm of other potential investors in future colonies.

Another obstacle to colonization was the charter that Queen Elizabeth had given Ralegh. As long as there was any hope that the Roanoke colonists survived, Ralegh retained the sole right to colonize North America. However, Ralegh could not convince investors to finance another venture to the New World.

OPPOSITE: *Nova Britannia* was a pamphlet issued in 1609 by the London Company in London to encourage people to invest and settle in a new colony in Virginia.

New King, Old Problems

As the 17th century began in England, the wool textile (cloth) industry in Europe expanded, increasing the push for private, enclosed lands where sheep could graze. Parliament (Britain's lawmaking body) passed several acts that allowed wealthy landowners to enclose public lands and raise sheep. Peasants who had once used that land to grow their food and graze their livestock found themselves with no way to feed their families. Faced with starvation, they sought work in towns and cities.

Few of the rural arrivals found work in the cities, however. Homeless, they turned to begging and stealing to survive. Once again, faraway Virginia seemed to hold the solution to England's problems. There, England's poor and homeless could provide the physical labor necessary to carve a colony out of the wilderness.

In 1606, a group of merchants formed the London Company. They proposed to King James that a new colony be established in Virginia. (Since Ralegh was now in prison, convicted of treason by James, he had lost the right to colonize North America.) The London Company would sell shares in the company to raise money for the venture. Some of the shareholders, as well as unemployed laborers, would make up the work force. Any profits would belong to the London Company's investors and the king.

treason—the crime of betraying one's country

King James granted the London Company a charter to settle an area stretching from present-day North Carolina to New York. The London Company could appoint a governing council for the colony, but the king had the final authority over the council.

This map shows the location of the 1585 Roanoke colony (in what is now North Carolina), and its distance from the Jamestown colony settled years later. Various Indian settlements in the region are also noted.

Armchair Adventurers

Once the charter was issued, the London Company set about raising money and finding men willing to settle in the Chesapeake Bay area of Virginia. People who invested their money in the company but had no desire to travel to the wilderness were called "adventurers." Men who wished to move to Virginia and actually settle the colony were known as "planters." The planters were basically employees of the London Company. None of these individuals, whether adventurers or planters, were granted ownership of any land in Virginia.

Some planters paid for their own voyages and supplies. In return, they would receive a share of any profits the company made. Other planters were indentured servants. These men agreed to work for the London Company in return for free passage to Virginia. At the end of their service—when they had fulfilled their contracts—they would be eligible to share in profits.

indentured servant—a person who agreed to work for a period of time, usually five to seven years, in exchange for paid passage to a colony

The Voyage

The 108 men who left London on December 20, 1606, were full of confidence. Advertisements for the new colony had lavishly praised the abundant resources of the New World. The failure of the Roanoke colony two decades earlier didn't seem to bother the settlers. They were headed to a different location. Most expected to find gold, as the Spanish had in South America, and get rich.

More than half of the colonists who set sail for Virginia that day listed their occupation as "gentleman." They may have been from well-to-do families, but most were younger sons who would not inherit any land if they remained in England. (At that time, only the oldest son inherited the family land). Four were boys—most likely orphans or runaways. Some were skilled tradesmen, such as carpenters, bricklayers, and blacksmiths. The rest were general laborers, soldiers, or indentured servants.

PACKING *for the* JOURNEY

THE COLONISTS WHO PAID FOR their own VOYAGE TO VIRGINIA were probably given lists of supplies that they would need to bring with them. None of these lists have been found. Supply lists for later colonists, however, provide a glimpse of the sorts of things each person would need in the new colony.

- CLOTHING, including one cap, three shirts, one wool suit, three pairs of stockings, and four pairs of shoes
- FOOD for one year, including 8 bushels (290 l) of grain, 2 bushels (72 l) of dried peas, and 1 gallon (3.8 l) of oil
- ARMS, including a musket, a sword, 20 pounds (9 kg) of gunpowder, and 60 pounds (27 kg) of lead shot
- TOOLS, including hoes, axes, handsaws, hammers, shovels, and nails
- HOUSEHOLD ITEMS, including one iron pot, one kettle, one frying pan, wooden dishes, and spoons
- MISCELLANEOUS ITEMS, such as fishing hooks and lines

Captain Christopher Newport led the voyage. It usually took about two months to reach North America. This time, however, storms kept blowing the ships back toward England. Finally, on April 26, 1607, the ships reached Chesapeake Bay. Three colonists died on the voyage. Another had been accused of mutiny for desiring to take over leadership of the expedition. He was now in chains.

mutiny—a refusal to obey a person in authority, with or without the use of force

Chesapeake Bay

Near the mouth of Chesapeake Bay, the men found meadows, wooded areas, and freshwater streams. George Percy, one of the gentlemen on board, said of the region, *"Upon this plot of ground we got good store of Mussels and Oysters . . . going a little further we [found] fine and beautifull Strawberries. . . ."*

The London Company had given Captain Newport a locked box that held the names of the men who would govern the colony, as well as the group's orders. After a few weeks of exploring, Captain Newport opened the box to learn that the man accused of mutiny—Captain John Smith—was a member of the governing council. Newport ordered that Smith be released from his chains.

The orders of the London Company said to find a good location for a fort around which they could build a settlement. The colonists were also directed to find a way for the London Company to make money in Virginia.

Jamestown

The new president of the governing council, Edward Maria Wingfield, led the colonists 60 miles (96 km) up the nearest river, which they named the James. When they reached a peninsula, they stopped to explore. The council decided to build the settlement there and call it Jamestown.

peninsula—land surrounded on three sides by water

The colonists had picked a bad spot to settle. A nearby marsh was thick with mosquitoes that carried malaria—a serious and sometimes deadly illness. The colonists' drinking water was frequently polluted with human waste and salt water, leading to disease.

Now, few men wanted to spend time building a fort or planting crops. Instead, they wanted to find the gold they believed was so plentiful. John Smith later wrote, "*There was no talke, no hope, nor worke, but dig gold, wash gold, [and] refine gold.*" A few weeks later, there was an Indian attack in which two colonists were killed. The remaining colonists quickly built James Fort.

After arriving in Virginia in 1607, the colonists built James Fort to protect their settlement and crops from Indian attacks.

PROFILE

Captain John Smith

The colonists who arrived in Chesapeake Bay in 1607 were thoroughly disgusted with one of the men who had made the journey. This man, John Smith, was only 25, yet he questioned the judgment of the older men. He also told wild stories about fighting the Turks and being captured and sold as a slave.

Luckily for the colonists, many of the stories Smith told were true (although he probably exaggerated a bit). The experience and skills he had gained in his travels, dealing with people from different cultures while fighting as a soldier for hire in France, Hungary, and Transylvania, proved invaluable in the New World.

Smith quickly assumed the primary responsibility for hunting, exploring the region, and trading with the Indians. Much of what we know today about the early years of Jamestown and the Indians in the area comes from books that Smith wrote. Smith's passion for this new land and his belief in its future made him an American hero.

THE POWHATAN CONFEDERACY

Although they didn't realize it, the Jamestown colonists had located their settlement in the middle of one of the most powerful Native American empires on the Atlantic coast. Known as the Powhatan Confederacy, the empire was ruled by Chief Wahunsunacock. About 30 Algonquian tribes, including the Powhatan, Potomac, Pamunkey, and Chickahominy, belonged to the confederacy.

The colonists referred to all the tribes in the empire as the Powhatan and even called Wahunsunacock "Chief Powhatan." Chief Powhatan's empire included about 200 villages. The village werowances were loyal to their tribal leaders, who were also called werowances. The tribal werowances, in turn, pledged loyalty to Chief Powhatan.

Powhatan Leaders

SCHOLARS ARE NOT SURE WHY Chief Powhatan allowed the English to settle at Jamestown when he easily could have destroyed them that first year. Some speculate that Powhatan hoped to convince the English to become allies in his wars against other Indian nations. Others note that the English provided a new source of copper, a metal that Powhatan valued highly.

After Powhatan's death in 1618, his brother Opechancanough became ruler of the empire. Under his leadership, the Powhatan launched two major attacks on the colonists, killing nearly 750 people. Opechancanough was finally captured in 1646, two years after the last massacre. At that time, he was nearly 100 years old. He was murdered by one of his prison guards.

Life in a Powhatan Village

Powhatan women built the longhouses, cooked meals, and made clothing. They also planted and tended corn, squash, beans, pumpkins, and tobacco. In addition, they gathered foods that grew wild, such as berries, apples, and nuts.

Powhatan men were skilled fishermen. They also hunted with bows and arrows. Bears, deer, rabbits, squirrels, and turkeys were favorite prey. When the men weren't hunting or fishing, they made dugout canoes from tree trunks. The dugouts required a great deal of effort to make, and each took several weeks to complete.

To build dugout canoes, Indians cut poplar logs in half and then cut grooves along the flat side. Burning embers were placed in the grooves to soften the wood, and seashells were used to dig out the inside of the log.

Powhatan children were expected to help the adults. Boys learned to shoot bows and arrows at a young age, and girls helped the women with farming and other chores.

Leisure time was an important part of the Powhatan culture. At night, people gathered in the center of the village to dance to the music of flutes, rattles, and drums. Athletic competitions such as foot races and wrestling matches were popular pastimes.

Powhatan Dress

In Virginia's coastal climate, Powhatan men and women wore little more than loincloths of animal skin most of the year. On really cold days, they wore other pieces of clothing made from animal skins.

Both men and women wore earrings and necklaces made of shells and beads. Women often tattooed their bodies for decoration, as well. Designs with flowers and animals were quite popular.

John Smith wrote of the Powhatan,

> *[The Powhatan Indians] adorne themselves most with copper beads and paintings. . . . In each eare commonly they have 3 great holes, whereat they hange chaines, bracelets, or copper. Some of their men weare in those holes, a smal greene and yellow coloured snake. . . . Others wear a dead Rat tied by the tail. Some on their heads weare the wing of a bird or some large feather, with a Rattell [a rattlesnake's rattle].*

King Powhatan comands C: Smith to be slayne his
daughter Pokahontas beggs his life his thankfullness
and how he Subiected 39 of their kings reade ye history

Struggle to Survive

STARVATION, DISEASE, AND CONFLICTS *with the Powhatan threaten the young colony.*

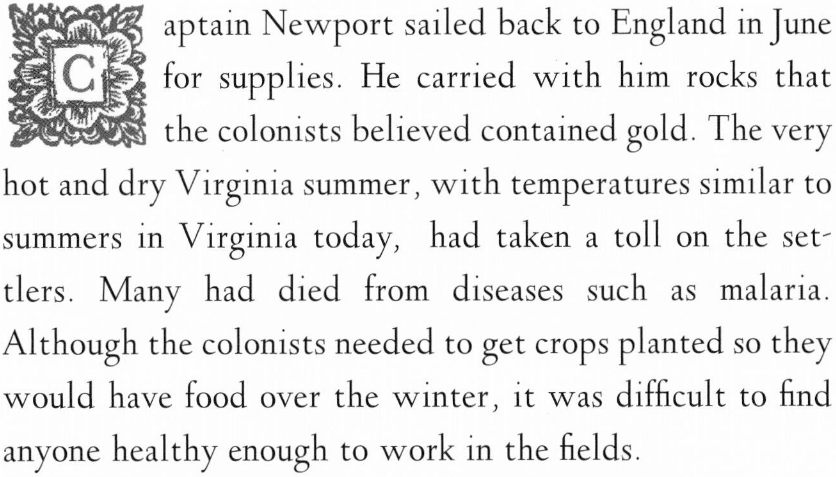

Captain Newport sailed back to England in June for supplies. He carried with him rocks that the colonists believed contained gold. The very hot and dry Virginia summer, with temperatures similar to summers in Virginia today, had taken a toll on the settlers. Many had died from diseases such as malaria. Although the colonists needed to get crops planted so they would have food over the winter, it was difficult to find anyone healthy enough to work in the fields.

OPPOSITE: This illustration from one of John Smith's books portrays Smith's version of how Pocahontas convinced her father, Chief Powhatan, to spare his life and form a truce with Virginia colonists.

A New Look at AN OLD BELIEF

UNTIL RECENTLY, MOST historians believed that food shortages faced by the colonists who settled Jamestown occurred because they had little farming experience or were too lazy to plant their own corn. New evidence uncovered by scientists offers another explanation, however. A second period of severe drought, like the one experienced two decades earlier by the settlers in Roanoke, began about the time the colonists arrived in Jamestown. Under these conditions, even the men's best efforts might not have produced enough food to sustain the colony.

By September, only 50 of the original 108 colonists were still alive. That month, George Percy wrote, "*Our men were destroyed with cruell diseases as Swellings, Fluxes [severe diarrhea], Burning Fevers . . . but for the most part they died of mere famine. . . . Thus, we lived for the space of five moneths in this miserable distresse.*"

CAPTURED BY THE INDIANS

In December, John Smith and two companions set off on a hunting trip. They soon walked into an Indian ambush. The men with him were killed, but Smith was captured by Chief Powhatan's brother, Opechancanough. Smith stalled his own execution by showing Opechancanough technical marvels such as his metal compass. Smith was held prisoner for several weeks. At times, he feared the tribe intended to eat him. Finally, Smith was taken to Werewocomoco, the home of Powhatan and his daughter, Pocahontas, who was about 11 years old.

In one of his later books, Smith wrote of the events that followed:

> *. . . two great stones were brought before Powhatan: then as many [warriors] as could layd hands on him [Smith], dragged him to [the stones], and thereon laid his head, and being ready with their clubs, to beate out his braines, Pocahontas, the Kings dearest daughter, when no intreaty could prevaile, got [Smith's] head in her armes and laid her owne upon his to save him from death: whereat the Emperour was contented he should live.*

The story of Pocahontas saving Smith is one of America's oldest legends. Smith didn't write about it in his early books on Virginia, although his later books include a detailed version. Some scholars believe the delay in writing this tale means it is not true. Historians do acknowledge that Pocahontas was a frequent visitor in Jamestown following Smith's release.

Some scholars believe that Powhatan didn't intend to kill Smith. Instead, they think the ritual showed that Powhatan intended to adopt Smith into the tribe. If this is true, Powhatan would have expected Smith and the colonists to pay tribute to him. Smith never realized this. The uneasy relationship between the Powhatan tribe and the colonists would continue until 1614.

A New Leader

When Smith finally returned to Jamestown in January 1608, he found only 38 men still alive. Newport arrived at the colony soon after Smith. He dropped off 108 new colonists and fresh supplies before returning to England.

Knowing that the new supplies wouldn't last, Smith sailed off to explore Chesapeake Bay and trade for food. Over the next several months, while exploring the Potomac, Rappahannock, Patapsco, and Susquehanna Rivers, Smith traded European finished goods, such as glass and copper beads, in exchange for corn with several tribes in the region.

This 1624 engraving from John Smith's book, *The Generall Historie of Virginia,* illustrates some of his experiences exploring and settling the Virginia colony.

Upon his return in September, Smith was elected president of Jamestown's governing council. Disgusted with the men who were more interested in finding gold than in ensuring a steady food supply, he immediately put a new rule into effect. All able-bodied men had to work at least six hours a day, either in the fields, gathering food, or building houses. To show that he meant it, Smith declared, "*He that will not work shall not eat.*" Smith's policy worked. Slowly, the colony grew more organized. Some hogs, brought from England by Newport and kept on a nearby island, also helped to create a more reliable food supply.

When Newport returned in October 1608, he brought 70 new colonists, including the first two women—Mrs. Thomas Forrest and her maid, Anne Burras. (Little is known about Mrs. Forrest, but Burras went on to marry carpenter John Laydon and have four daughters with him.) Newport also carried bad news. The rocks that the colonists had thought contained gold were worthless. The London Company sent a letter to the governing council. Alarmed by the expenses of sending food, tools, clothing, and other supplies, the company threatened to abandon the colonists in Virginia if they didn't discover gold or find at least one survivor of the Lost Colony soon. The company had hoped to incorporate any remaining members of the Lost Colony into their own settlement and use the survivors' knowledge and skills to help ensure the success of the new colony.

Smith sent an angry letter back, pointing out that the colonists were lucky to be alive after the hardships they had faced. Then he pleaded for the company to send skilled tradesmen to the colony, rather than young gentlemen who were not used to working: "*I entreat you rather send but thirty carpenters, husbandmen, gardeners, fishermen, blacksmiths, masons and diggers of trees' roots, well provided, than a thousand such as we have.*"

The Starving Time

In August 1609, a fleet brought about 400 new colonists to Virginia, raising the population to about 500. Soon after their arrival, Smith severely injured his leg in a gunpowder accident. When it didn't heal, he was forced to return to England for medical treatment.

George Percy took over as president of the colony after Smith left. Unfortunately, Percy was not a strong leader. The discipline that Smith had forced upon the colonists soon disappeared. Relations with the Powhatan worsened when the settlers threatened to use force to make the Indians give them food rather than trading for it.

Tired of the English threats, the Powhatan began attacking settlers who ventured out of the fort that winter. The Indians also killed the colonists' livestock. Afraid to leave the fort, the colonists soon ran out of food and firewood. They tore down their houses and burned the wood to keep warm. Survivors told of eating "*horses and other beastes as long as they Lasted.*" They then turned to "*doggs Catts Ratts and myce.*" Colonists lucky enough to have leather boots or shoes ate those. A few brave souls sneaked outside the fort to search for snakes and roots to eat. One man was later convicted of murder for killing his wife and eating her. He was sentenced to death.

Only 65 colonists survived until the next English supply ship arrived in May 1610. The crew agreed to take the survivors back to England. Before they reached Chesapeake Bay, however, they met three English ships. On board one of the ships was Sir Thomas West, Lord De La Warr, the newly appointed governor of Virginia. Unbeknownst to the colonists, the London Company—now known as the Virginia Company—had decided to replace the president and governing council with a governor.

New Hope for the Colony

Lord De La Warr brought 300 new settlers with him. After demanding that the ship with the surviving settlers return to Jamestown, De La Warr set about restoring order in the colony. He soon established the "Articles, Lawes, and Orders, Divine, Politique, and Martiall for the Colony in Virginea."

These strict laws addressed every aspect of life in the colony. The punishment for breaking a law was swift and harsh. Colonists could be sentenced to death for many crimes, including running away from the colony, speaking out against God, the king, or the Virginia Company—even for stealing grapes. Several of the new laws helped improve relations with Native Americans in the region. Taking anything away from the Indians by force was now punishable by death, as was the burning of Indian villages or storehouses (except as ordered by an officer).

Soldiers made the colonists obey the new laws, and slowly, conditions improved. Diseases still caused many deaths, but few colonists died of starvation under De La Warr's strict command. De La Warr himself became very ill and returned to England in 1611.

The next governor, Sir Thomas Dale, continued to rule with a stern hand. Under his leadership, three new settlements were established; Henrico, Kecoughtan (present-day Hampton), and Charles City. Jamestown became the capital of the colony.

In 1612, a colonist named John Rolfe tried an experiment that finally transformed Virginia into a profitable colony. Rolfe had obtained some West Indian tobacco seeds on the island of Trinidad during his initial voyage to Virginia. Spanish colonies in the West Indies were known for their fine tobacco. Once in Virginia, Rolfe planted the West Indian tobacco seeds instead of the wild tobacco grown by the Powhatan. The resulting crop was widely regarded as superior in taste to the wild tobacco. When Rolfe sent his first shipment of tobacco to England in 1613, it found a ready market.

The habit of smoking tobacco was gaining popularity in Europe. Although King James believed that smoking was "*a custom loathsome to the eye, hateful to the nose, harmful to the brain, [and] dangerous to the lungs,*" he allowed the colonists to grow and sell tobacco. He could not resist the opportunity to make a lot of money.

Also in 1613, Pocahontas was taken hostage by a colonist who intended to trade her for English settlers being held by the Powhatan. Rolfe met Pocahontas while she was a captive. They fell in love and married when she was freed in 1614. Their marriage launched a period of peace between the colonists and the Powhatan.

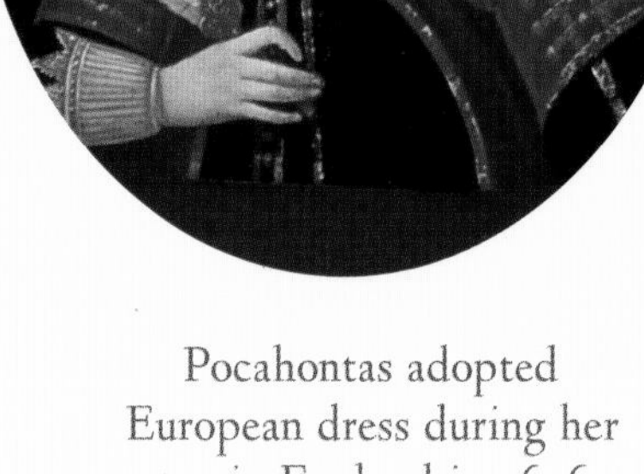

Pocahontas adopted European dress during her stay in England in 1616.

Improved Living

Soon, hundreds of acres were cleared and planted with tobacco. In 1615, the colonists shipped slightly more than 1 ton (0.9 mt) of tobacco to England. This increased to 10 tons

(9 mt) within three years. As tobacco grew in value, colonists often used the leaves in place of money. Tobacco became known as "green gold."

In 1619, the Virginia Company revised its policies and allowed colonists to own land. Investors were granted 100 acres (40 ha) of land, while each colonist who paid for the voyage received 50 acres (20 ha). A family of four who paid for its passage would receive 200 acres (80 ha). Even indentured servants were promised 50 acres upon fulfilling their contracts.

The Virginia Company also announced the creation of the Virginia General Assembly. While the governor would still rule Virginia, the General Assembly would write the laws. This legislative body was made up of the Governor's Council and the House of Burgesses. Gentlemen were appointed to the Governor's Council by the governor,

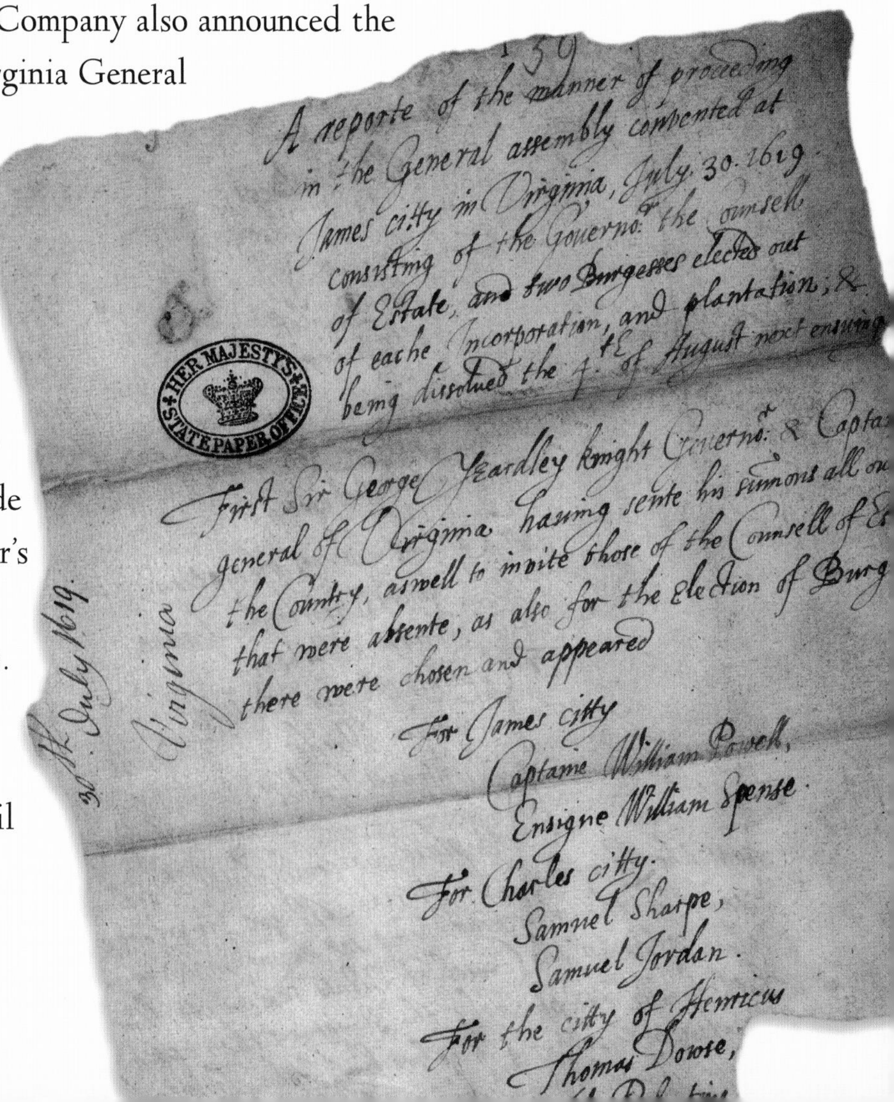
159
A reporte of the manner of proceeding
in the General assembly convented at
James citty in Virginia, July 30. 1619
consisting of the Governor the Counsell
of Estate, and two Burgesses elected out
of eache Incorporation, and plantation, &
being dissolved the 4th of August next ensuing
First Sir George Yeardley knight Governor & Capta
general of Virginia having sente his summons all ou
the Country, aswell to invite those of the Counsell of Es
that were absente, as also for the Election of Burg
there were chosen and appeared
For James citty
Captaine William Powell,
Ensigne William Spense.
For Charles citty
Samuel Sharpe,
Samuel Jordan.
For the citty of Henricus
Thomas Dowse,

30th July 1619
Virginia

HER MAJESTY'S STATE PAPER OFFICE

but representatives to the House of Burgesses were elected by white male landowners. The house could pass laws, but these had to be approved by both the governor and the Governor's Council. The house formed a solid foundation for representative government in the Colonies.

Legislating Common Sense

ONE PROBLEM IN COLONIAL VIRGINIA WAS THE CONTINUED reliance of the colonists on the Indians for food. Few people wanted to plant food crops when they could plant tobacco and make money. As a result, armed colonists often forced Indians to give them food. One of the first laws passed by the General Assembly required landowners to grow enough food to support their families, as well as any servants.

After these changes, immigration to Virginia exploded. In 1619 alone, more than 1,200 people arrived in the colony. More land was needed to support the new arrivals, and tensions with the Indians began to increase once again. ⁂

OPPOSITE: Written on this time-worn piece of paper is the list of burgesses elected to the first General Assembly of Jamestown in 1619.

CHAPTER FOUR

Changing Times

The Navigation Acts *cause tobacco prices to drop as rebellion spreads fear and slavery increases.*

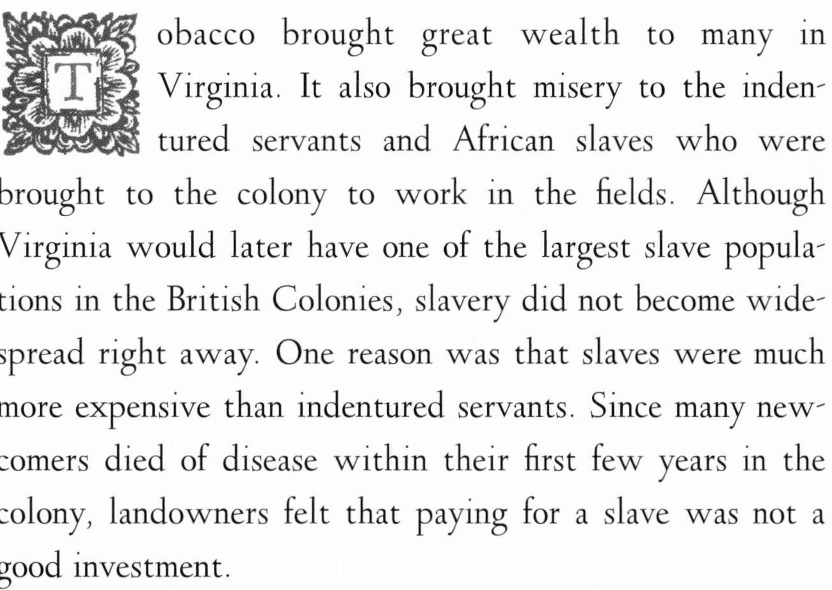

Tobacco brought great wealth to many in Virginia. It also brought misery to the indentured servants and African slaves who were brought to the colony to work in the fields. Although Virginia would later have one of the largest slave populations in the British Colonies, slavery did not become widespread right away. One reason was that slaves were much more expensive than indentured servants. Since many newcomers died of disease within their first few years in the colony, landowners felt that paying for a slave was not a good investment.

OPPOSITE: This 1700 woodcut illustrates tobacco plantation owners relaxing while slaves toil in the fields.

The first Africans arrived in Virginia on a Dutch ship in August 1619. From all accounts, these first 20 Africans were indentured servants. Once they had fulfilled their contracts, they were treated like any other indentured servants, receiving land, clothing, and tools with their freedom. Some went on to buy indentured servants of their own.

The Powhatan Strike Back

By 1622, the colony had expanded far beyond the original Jamestown settlement. Plantations were beginning to develop to the north, along the eastern shore of Chesapeake Bay. The Powhatan were being pushed from their lands to make room for more Europeans.

plantation—a large estate or farm where crops are raised, often by resident workers

Following Chief Powhatan's death in 1618, his brother Opechancanough ruled the Powhatan Confederacy. Opechancanough resented the continuous expansion of the colony. In front of the settlers, he and his followers hid their bitterness, but in reality, they were planning a surprise attack.

On March 22, 1622, warriors visited outlying plantations and settlements, just as they had been doing for years. The unsuspecting colonists welcomed the Indians. At a specified time, the Powhatan attacked. Sometimes using the settlers' own weapons and tools, the Native Americans killed nearly 350 colonists and burned many plantations. The death toll might have been higher had settlers in Jamestown not been forewarned of the attack by an Indian boy named Chango.

Opechancanough probably wanted to frighten the English into leaving Virginia for good. Instead, the colonists sought revenge. The settlers demolished canoes, tore up village temples, and killed any Indians they met. Just before the fall harvest, Indian villages and cornfields were burned.

In 1622 Chief Opechancanough of the Powhatan ordered a surprise attack on the colonists who had settled the areas surrounding Jamestown. The Indians were angry that their lands were being taken over by settlers.

The following spring, English leaders invited Opechancanough and his warriors to join them for peace talks. As the discussion ended, the English offered poisoned wine to the Native Americans. As the Indians fell over, the colonists attacked, killing most of them. Opechancanough was one of the few who escaped.

A Royal Colony

King James blamed the high death rates of settlers on poor management by the Virginia Company. His solution was to make Virginia a royal colony in 1624. This meant that the king, rather than the company, would make all the decisions about the colony.

King Charles I restored the Virginia House of Burgesses in 1625.

One of the first things King James did was to disband the House of Burgesses. However, the burgesses continued to meet unofficially. The house was restored to the General Assembly a year later, when James died and his successor, Charles I, recognized the representative body. This official recognition was, at least in part, King Charles's acceptance of the colonists' right to limited self-government.

By 1640, there were about 10,000 colonists living in the Tidewater region. They outnumbered Native Americans two to one. Opechancanough led another large-scale attack against the English in 1644, hoping to drive them from America forever. This time, 400 settlers were massacred.

Once again, the English set out to destroy Indian villages in Virginia. Few Powhatan escaped the slaughter. Most of those who did fled west or north to live with other Indian tribes. The once-mighty Powhatan Confederacy was shattered. Hoping to prevent future massacres of colonists, the General Assembly passed a law allowing colonists to kill any Indians who visited a settlement without permission.

SETTLING THE FRONTIER

The Powhatan and neighboring tribes had been pushed from the prime land bordering the James, York, Rappahannock, and Potomac Rivers. In their place, colonists with money and political connections had established some of Virginia's largest plantations.

This coastal land, known as the Tidewater region, gave farmers the ability to load tobacco directly onto ships that anchored near the plantations. Another advantage was the region's relative safety. By 1650, the Powhatan tribes had been driven out of Tidewater Virginia or confined to a small reservation. The Tidewater region was also the first stop for new immigrants. Their arrival made it fairly easy for landowners to find indentured servants to help farm their plantations.

By the mid-17th century, most of Tidewater Virginia was privately owned. When indentured servants completed their contracts, they were entitled to 50 acres (20 ha). However, there was no land nearby for them to claim. The freedmen had a choice. They could become tenant farmers on large plantations and never own land, or they could claim their own farms on the sparsely settled region west of the Tidewater. On the frontier, they would have to fend off frequent Indian attacks, cultivate less fertile land due to rockier soil and fewer river floodplains, and pay higher costs to transport their tobacco to market.

freedman—an indentured servant who has gained freedom after completing the terms of his or her contract

tenant farmer—a farmer who rents land to cultivate

frontier—wilderness that borders a settled area

Despite these difficulties, the dream of owning their own land led many freedmen to settle on the frontier. They believed that if they worked hard, they would be successful. However, these small independent farmers slowly grew resentful of the wealthy elite.

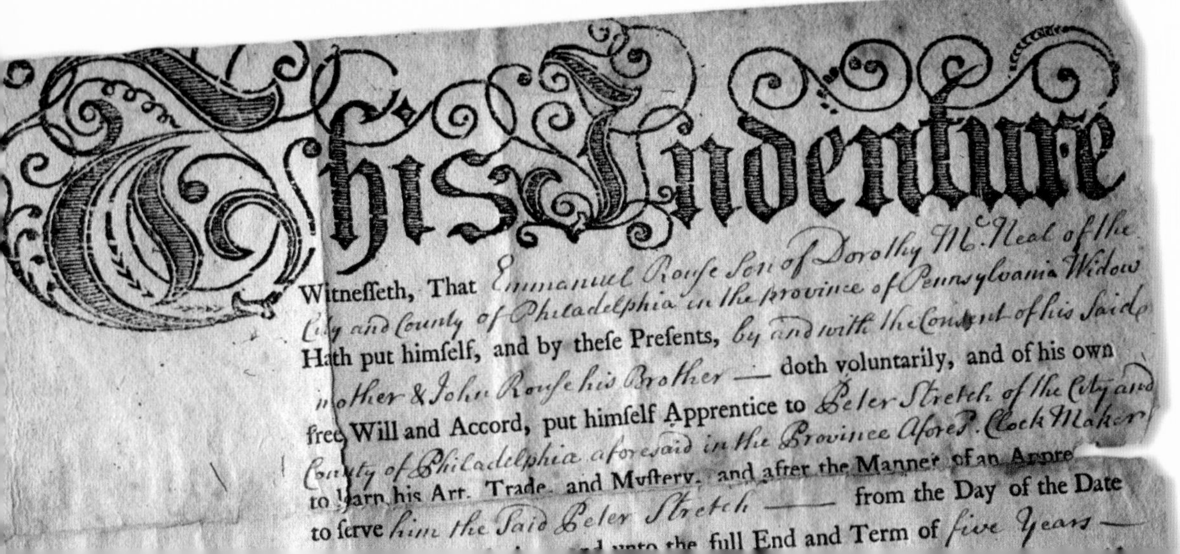

This Indenture

Witneſſeth, That Emmanuel Rouſe Son of Dorothy McNeal of the City and County of Philadelphia in the Province of Pennsylvania Widow Hath put himſelf, and by theſe Preſents, by and with the Conſent of his Said Mother & John Rouſe his Brother — doth voluntarily, and of his own free Will and Accord, put himſelf Apprentice to Peter Stretch of the City and County of Philadelphia aforesaid in the Province Afores^d. Clock Maker to learn his Art, Trade, and Myſtery, and after the Manner of an Appre[ntice] to ſerve him the Said Peter Stretch —— from the Day of the Date ... unto the full End and Term of five Years —

Trouble Ahead

In 1651, Parliament passed the first Navigation Act. This law was intended to force colonists to sell their products only to British merchants. Before the law had passed, merchants had been coming from a variety of places to buy the premium Virginia tobacco. For example, in 1649, unknown *"men of worth and credit"* from Virginia noted that *"at last Christmas we had trading here ten ships from London, two from Bristoll, twelve Hollanders, and seven from New-England."*

The first Navigation Act was not enforced, but Parliament passed other Navigation Acts after Charles II took the throne in 1660. Within a few years, British merchants had control of Virginia's tobacco exports. The price of tobacco in the Colonies plunged to one-fourth its former level. British merchants still charged high prices when they sold the tobacco in England, but the profits now went into the merchants' pockets rather than the growers.

The Navigation Acts had a devastating effect on Virginia's economy. Tenant farmers were unable to pay their rents. Many small landowners were forced to sell their land and possessions to pay off debts. The gentry often bought this land at very low prices. Governor William Berkeley observed that small landowners earned *"soe very little for their labores as it will not cloath them and their Families."*

gentry—members of the upper class

OPPOSITE: In this contract, called an indenture, a newly arrived immigrant agrees to work as a clock worker's apprentice, or indentured servant, for five years.

Most colonists believed that it was dangerous to criticize the Navigation Acts publicly. Even the usually vocal House of Burgesses stayed quiet. The members knew they had no power to change things and feared arrest if they spoke out. Many Virginians felt powerless—one writer described the laws as *"an Evil we with Patience now must bear, as we have it not in our Power to avoid or prevent it."*

Due to the Navigation Acts, for the first time, it cost more money to raise tobacco than the growers made when they sold it. To control costs, some owners of large plantations started using slaves instead of indentured servants in their tobacco fields. Slaves had to work their entire lifetimes without pay, rather than the five to seven years of an indentured servant's contract. The children of slaves were also slaves, providing a ready-made labor force. In order to remain competitive, small landowners slowly began switching to slave labor, too.

Bacon's Rebellion

The small landowners and tenant farmers who lived on the western frontier placed much of the blame for their misery on the wealthy plantation owners. Since the establishment of the General Assembly in 1619, the men on the Governor's Council, as well as those elected to the House of Burgesses, had been selected from the gentry. Over the next five and a half decades, these men regularly voted themselves large salaries, reduced the taxes that large landowners paid, and raised taxes on small landowners. With each new privilege that the elite granted themselves, the resentment grew for freedmen who were struggling to get by.

The conflict between freedmen and gentry came to a head in the 1670s. The problems began with a trading dispute between a settler and a group of Susquehanna Indians. The fighting soon sparked Indian raids throughout the frontier. The people living on the frontier asked Governor Berkeley to send a military officer to lead them against the Susquehanna and other Indian tribes, but he refused. The governor even refused to let the settlers organize their own militia to fight the Indians. Berkeley was afraid that attacks by the settlers would cause all the Indian tribes in the region to join together against the colonists. He also worried that the "rabble" making up this militia would attack the wealthy plantation owners or the governor himself.

militia—a group of citizen-soldiers

One member of the Governor's Council, Nathaniel Bacon, had a large plantation on the frontier. A fairly recent immigrant from England, Bacon believed that "*all Indians in generall...were all Enemies.*" When Berkeley refused to support the frontier planters, Bacon stepped forward to lead them. They marched through Virginia, killing both peaceful and hostile Indians. Berkeley charged Bacon and his followers with treason, a crime that was punishable by death.

In July 1676, Bacon led his followers to Middle Plantation (later Williamsburg). There, he issued a Declaration of the People, criticizing Berkeley's government. Bacon demanded lower taxes and better land for freedmen. He placed the blame for launching a civil war upon Berkeley's shoulders. Most of the colonists agreed with Bacon and signed an oath denouncing Berkeley.

In September, Bacon and his followers marched to Jamestown. Berkeley fled the city and Bacon burned the town to the ground. Then the rebels gleefully ransacked the plantations of Berkeley's supporters. A month later, Bacon died suddenly after a bout of the "bloody flux". The rebellion died with him, and Berkeley returned to Jamestown, which was being rebuilt.

When the governor of Virginia refused to help defend western farmers against Indian attack, Nathaniel Bacon led the frontier planters in a battle against both peaceful and hostile Indians. This 1676 uprising became known as Bacon's Rebellion.

After the Rebellion

King Charles II believed that the Virginia government's unfair laws had led to Bacon's Rebellion. In 1677, Charles sent a new governor—Sir Herbert Jeffreys—to Virginia, along with orders to pardon the rebels. Berkeley refused to step down as governor. He had 23 leaders of the rebellion hanged—after the king had pardoned them. Four months later, under pressure from the English government and Virginia colonists, Berkeley finally gave up his position to Jeffreys and returned to England.

Fearful of another revolt, the gentry began to limit the number of indentured servants who immigrated to Virginia. As a result, the gentry began to embrace slavery. Eventually, servants were replaced by African slaves. By 1750, an additional 40,000 slaves had been brought to the colony, and nearly all field workers were slaves.

As the colonists became more dependent upon slave labor, the fear of slave uprisings created stronger alliances between white Virginians of all economic levels. In addition, the gentry-controlled General Assembly passed several laws during the 1690s and early 1700s that reduced taxes, allowed all white men to vote whether they were landowners or not, and enabled frontier families to protect themselves from Indian attacks. These changes encouraged whites at all economic levels to think of themselves as Virginians rather than English citizens. ⁂

Westward Expansion

New ideas arrive *in Virginia, along with thousands of new settlers.*

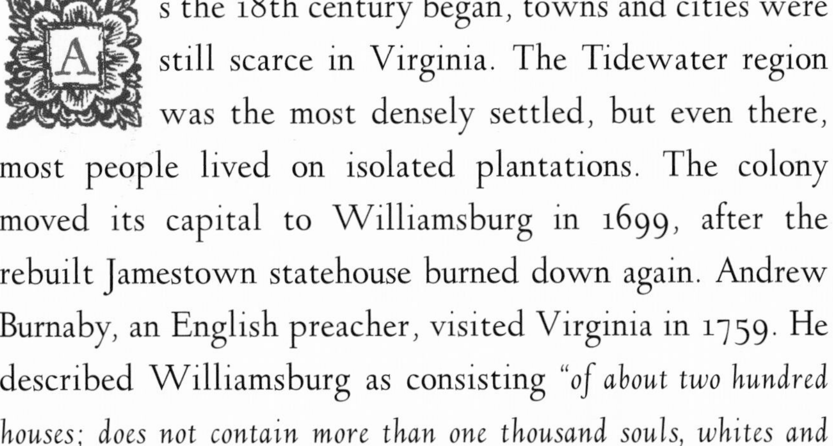

As the 18th century began, towns and cities were still scarce in Virginia. The Tidewater region was the most densely settled, but even there, most people lived on isolated plantations. The colony moved its capital to Williamsburg in 1699, after the rebuilt Jamestown statehouse burned down again. Andrew Burnaby, an English preacher, visited Virginia in 1759. He described Williamsburg as consisting *"of about two hundred houses; does not contain more than one thousand souls, whites and negroes; and is far from being a place of any consequence."*

OPPOSITE: In 1716, Alexander Spotswood led an expedition to explore the Blue Ridge mountains. He and his men became known as the Knights of the Golden Horseshoe.

Two times a year, Virginians who had business to conduct before the court or government, left their plantations and farms and traveled to Williamsburg for Publick Times. On these occasions, the General Assembly met at the capitol, trials were held in the courthouse, and men met to conduct business. Taverns were filled as planters discussed the latest political developments or talked about tobacco production.

After living on isolated plantations for much of the year, people were ready to socialize during Publick Times. They attended balls, watched horse races, and laughed at puppet shows. Williamsburg's merchants were kept busy as wealthy planters and their families shopped for luxuries and the latest fashions.

Publick Times were cause for celebration and dancing for the farm families who lived far from the more populated towns of the Tidewater region.

STRANGE Bedfellows

MOST OF THE PEOPLE TRAVELING TO WILLIAMSBURG FOR Publick Times found lodging at taverns. Unlike today's hotels, the taverns provided a place to sleep but offered little privacy. They certainly didn't guarantee comfort. Men staying at a tavern might find themselves sleeping crossways in a bed with four or more other men who were in town for the political events. Rich planters in the finest clothes might find themselves next to poor farmers wearing homespun. People shrugged off the inconvenience, saying,

Politics makes strange bedfellows.

SOUTH FROM PENNSYLVANIA

Immigrants continued to pour into Virginia, and they all wanted land. Although land could be purchased in the Tidewater region or the Piedmont, it was expensive. (The Piedmont is the region of rolling hills in central Virginia that stretches west from the Tidewater to the foothills of the Blue Ridge mountains.) The sheer number of newcomers and the demand for cheaper land caused the colony to expand even farther west.

In 1716, Governor Alexander Spotswood and a group of friends set off to explore the Blue Ridge mountains, where they found rushing rivers and lush valleys. To commemorate the journey, Spotswood gave each member of the expedition a golden horseshoe. They became known as the Knights of the Golden Horseshoe.

Many of Virginia's wealthy planters were also land speculators. After Spotswood's expedition to the Blue Ridge mountains, they began buying large tracts of land there. They would then divide the tracts into smaller plots and offer them for sale. A natural pathway that later became known as the Great Wagon Road led from Pennsylvania into the valleys of Virginia. As a result, much of the Shenandoah Valley was settled by German and Scotch-Irish immigrants from Pennsylvania. Families from France, the Netherlands, Switzerland, and Sweden also settled in the new frontier.

land speculator—a person who purchases land to sell for a profit

Scotch-Irish—Scottish people who had settled in Northern Ireland for a time before migrating to America

Virginia's population tripled between 1700 and 1750, and Virginians continued to look westward for new land to settle. This time the goal was Ohio Country, which lay beyond the Appalachian Mountains. The growing demand to settle this fertile hunting ground of the Cherokee and other Native Americans would create new headaches for the king and the Virginia land speculators.

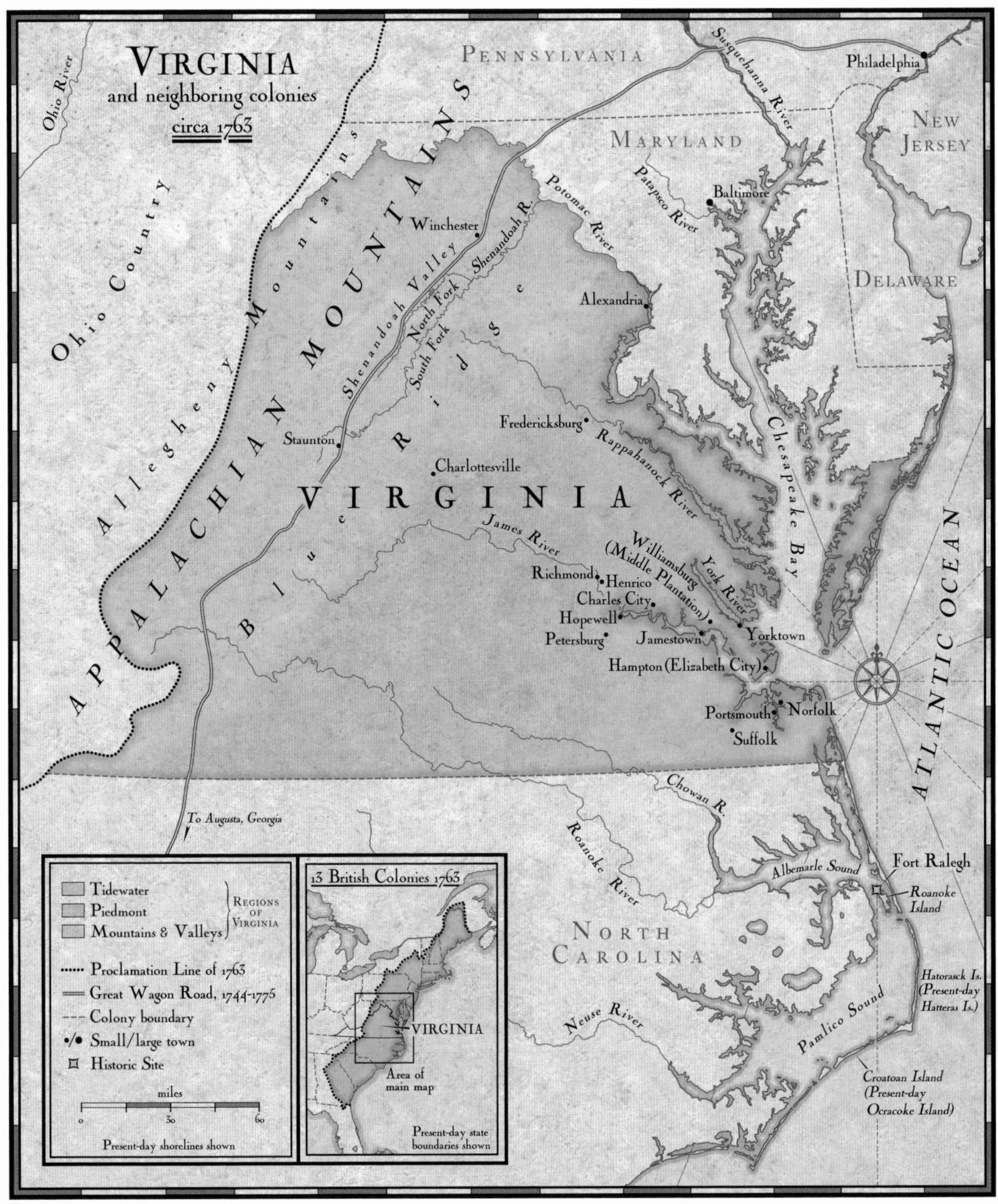

European settlement in Virginia began in the Tidewater region (pink area) and spread west, first to Piedmont (green area) and then to the mountains and valleys beyond (tan area). After the French and Indian War, the British established the Proclamation Line of 1763 (dotted black line) as the boundary between its colonies and Indian lands.

George Whitefield, a traveling minister who spoke to people wherever they gathered, preached the need for spiritual conversion during a period in the early 18th century known as the Great Awakening.

The Great Awakening

Early colonists traveled to Virginia in search of wealth rather than religious freedom, but religion did play an important role in the development of the colony. The Anglican Church, or Church of England, had become the state church in the early 1620s, when Virginia became a royal colony. Colonists were required to support the Anglican Church with their taxes, no matter what faith they practiced. Anyone who held public office had to be a member of the Anglican Church.

Despite this government support for Anglicanism, colonists in Virginia were allowed to practice other Protestant religions. Those who did so were known as dissenters. These non-Anglicans were required to register with the courts. Dissenters also had to purchase special licenses in order to hold services. Very few dissenters lived in Virginia until the mid-18th century.

dissenter—the Anglican Church's term for a person who practiced another religion

During the 1730s and 1740s, evangelical preachers such as George Whitefield sparked a series of religious revivals in New England. They preached a revolutionary message—that a person's public church affiliation mattered less than the private experience of spiritual conversion. This period became known as the Great Awakening. The Awakening reached Virginia in the late 1740s, when Samuel Davies and other evangelical preachers arrived in the region.

Presbyterian, Methodist, and Baptist leaders found eager converts on Virginia's frontier. The Scotch-Irish and German settlers there had few ties to the Anglican Church. Indeed, there were few churches of any kind in the wilderness.

After 1750, many evangelical Christians began preaching to slaves. Evangelicals believed that everyone was equal in the eyes of God, whether white or black, slave or free. By the late eighteenth century, most followers of evangelical religions considered slavery a sin.

evangelical—Protestants who believe in the ultimate authority of the Bible and experience a personal conversion to Christianity

Colonial Life

From the plantation to the frontier, *life is harder for some white Virginians than for others.*

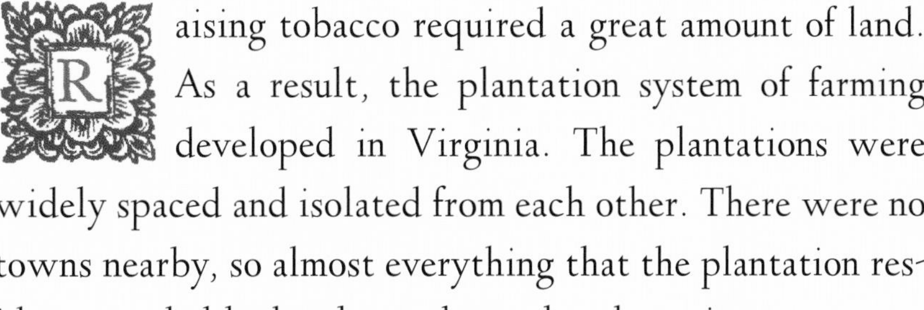

Raising tobacco required a great amount of land. As a result, the plantation system of farming developed in Virginia. The plantations were widely spaced and isolated from each other. There were no towns nearby, so almost everything that the plantation residents needed had to be made on the plantation.

For many years, plantation houses were small wooden structures. Most white people who came to the colony in the early years hoped to get rich quickly and then return home to England. They didn't want to build grand houses if they weren't going to stay and live in them.

The children and grandchildren of these first plantation owners were different. They considered Virginia their home. As their wealth grew, they built luxurious mansions

OPPOSITE: A 1730 painting by English artist Charles Phillips shows a colonial Williamsburg family in the living room of their lavish plantation home.

overlooking the rivers of the Tidewater region. These 18th-century homes were usually made of brick. Trees lined the long drives that led up to the houses. The interiors were decorated with the finest furnishings from Europe.

The men and women of the gentry could afford to buy elegant clothes. Men dressed up in fine woolen or silk suits. Ruffles, laces, and bows added a fashionable flourish. Wigs—made from goat, horse, yak, or human hair—were worn on formal occasions. Women wore gowns made from rich silk brocades and other fine fabrics. Petticoats, stockings, shoes, and other accessories were often imported.

Given the distance from one plantation to another, most socializing took place during extended visits to a neighbor's plantation. When Andrew Burnaby traveled through Virginia in 1759, he found the Virginians he met to be *"indolent, easy, and good-natured; extremely fond of society, and much given to convivial pleasures."* Dances were quite popular, and Burnaby noted that the women were *"immoderately fond of dancing, and indeed it is almost the only amusement they partake of."* Men enjoyed horse races, cards, and hunting during their leisure time.

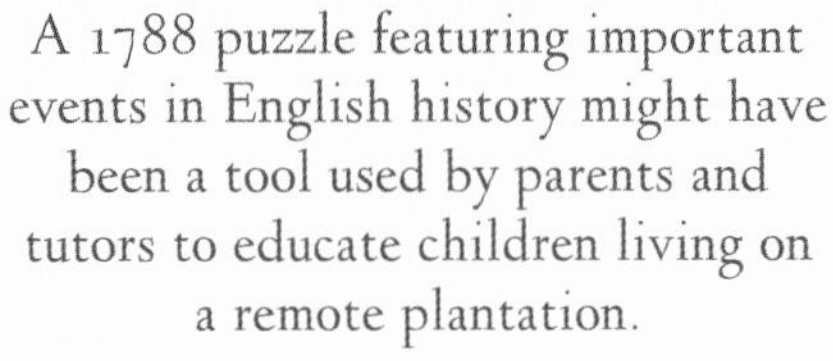

A 1788 puzzle featuring important events in English history might have been a tool used by parents and tutors to educate children living on a remote plantation.

Childhood on the Plantation

Children of wealthy landowners had plenty of leisure time, as slaves took care of most of the chores on the plantation. In this painting a young boy plays with a top.

Unlike white children who lived on the frontier or black children in slavery, children of plantation owners didn't have to work. They had time to play with their fine china tea sets and toy soldiers. Servants or slaves made sure the children were dressed and fed each morning, and they put the children to bed each night.

Most children of plantation owners received an education of some sort. Since there were few schools in the colony, parents either taught their children to read and cipher or hired a tutor. Boys were more likely than girls to receive an education, although girls were often included in the classes when a tutor was available. Girls were not taught advanced mathematics or foreign languages, however. In those days, few people believed girls could master these and other difficult subjects.

cipher—to perform basic math calculations such as adding and subtracting

tutor—a private teacher

Philip Vickers Fithian, a private tutor, kept a detailed journal of his time with the Robert Carter family at a plantation called Nomini Hall. He taught *"eight of Mr. Carters Sons—One Nephew—And five Daughters."* The subjects included English, mathematics, and spelling.

Aside from formal learning, children were expected to learn to ride horses and dance. Girls often received music and art lessons. They also spent time each day mastering handiwork such as sewing and embroidery.

A typical school day started around 6 a.m. with a lesson. Breakfast was at 8, with classes from 9 until noon. Then the children had a break until dinner, which was usually about 2 p.m. The last lessons of the day were taught from 3 to 6. Supper was served at 8:30 or 9 p.m.

Boys had the opportunity to further their education as they got older. While the wealthiest planters sometimes sent their sons to England to attend university, many young men attended the College of William and Mary in Williamsburg, founded in 1693. The College of New Jersey, which would later be renamed Princeton University, also attracted many students from Virginia.

Life on a Small Farm

Like the wealthy plantation owners, small landowners were isolated from their neighbors and forced to be self-sufficient. Most small landowners lived in simple wooden houses that they built themselves. These farmers also made most of their furniture. They purchased supplies such as nails and wooden casks for shipping tobacco from merchants in Williamsburg and other towns.

Much of the farm family's day was consumed by work. Some small landowners had servants or slaves to help them with the backbreaking work in the tobacco fields. In addition, farmers often raised cattle, hogs, and poultry. There were cows to milk, eggs to gather, and butter to make. In the fall, hogs and cattle were butchered to provide meat for the winter. Cowhide was turned into leather for shoes. Families made their own soap, candles, tools, and other necessities.

In addition to tobacco and other cash crops, farmers grew a variety of food crops. These included wheat, carrots, onions, potatoes, and corn. Some farmers tended fruit orchards. Berries, nuts, wild game, and fish added variety to meals.

The clothing worn by farm families was not nearly as fancy as that of the gentry. The women and girls in the family sewed most of the family's clothes. Linen and woolen fabrics were usually purchased from weavers in nearby settlements, but some women made their own. Cotton fabric was imported from England.

Women living along the frontier tended to the home and care and feeding of their family. In this engraving, a colonial woman has gathered vegetables from her garden and is carrying them back to her cabin home in the basket on her head.

Childhood on the Farm

The children living on farms had daily chores. They weeded gardens, tended crops, and took care of the livestock. Girls helped their mothers with the cooking and sewing. Boys hunted and helped their fathers in the field.

Even though there was a lot of work, children usually found time to play. Many of the games they enjoyed, like hopscotch, are still played today. Toys such as tops and dolls were homemade. In the evenings, family members might challenge each other with riddles or puzzles.

Farm children rarely received a formal education. If their parents were able to read, write, and cipher, they taught their children these skills. Otherwise, the children grew up uneducated.

Life on the Frontier

The many skills necessary for a frontier family to thrive were outlined in 1711 by Reverend John Urmstone. He wrote, "*Men are generally carpenters, joiners, wheelwrights, coopers, butchers . . . shoemakers, tallow-chandlers, watermen, and what not; women soap-makers, starch-makers, dyers, etc.*"

The first job on the frontier was to build a house. Scotch-Irish families usually shaped logs into one-room cabins. The

cooper—a person who makes barrels

tallow-chandler—a person who makes or sells candles and soaps created from the melted fat of cattle and sheep

Germans preferred to build stone houses. Each house had a fireplace, used both for cooking and for heating the house. Once the house was complete, the men and boys would begin crafting the furniture.

Many settlers didn't have horses or oxen to pull tree stumps out of the ground, so they left them there. Crops were planted around the stumps until the stumps finally rotted. While most of the settlers' energy went to growing food, most colonists planted at least some tobacco.

Frontier settlers had to be skilled with guns. Their families relied on wild game, including rabbit, squirrels, deer, and bears, for food. Settlers also had to be ready to protect their livestock from wolves and defend themselves against an Indian attack.

Because they were so isolated, frontier families gathered with their neighbors when a family had a task that was too big to do on its own, like building a house or barn. While the men were putting the building up, the women would work on quilts and prepare the meals.

Children growing up on the frontier lived lives very similar to those of farm children. Frontier families were usually large, so the older children were responsible for helping to care for the younger ones. Their parents depended upon them to do daily chores, as well. When they did have free time, the children entertained themselves. They made toys from wood scraps and dolls from rags or cornhusks. ※

Servants and Slaves in Virginia

VIRGINIA'S GENTRY *cherishes the idea of freedom yet embraces slavery.*

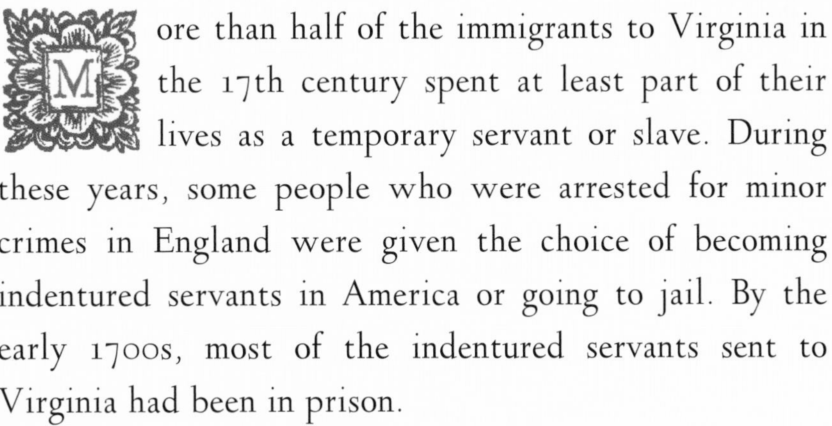

More than half of the immigrants to Virginia in the 17th century spent at least part of their lives as a temporary servant or slave. During these years, some people who were arrested for minor crimes in England were given the choice of becoming indentured servants in America or going to jail. By the early 1700s, most of the indentured servants sent to Virginia had been in prison.

OPPOSITE: In this 18th-century engraving of a tobacco farm in Virginia, a slave family is shown sorting and hanging tobacco leaves.

In the early years, indentured servants worked for the Virginia Company. Later, the servants' contracts were owned by individuals. Adult servants agreed to work for a period of years, usually five to seven. Children who came to America as indentured servants were freed when they turned 21. In return, the employer paid for their passage to the New World and provided for their daily needs. (Passage usually cost about a year's wages for the English poor.) At the end of their contracts, the servants would receive "freedom dues" of some sort—usually food, clothing, and tools. After 1619, some indentured servants were given land as part of their freedom dues.

Female convicts arriving in Virginia to work as indentured servants were often married off to settlers living on frontier farms in need of a partner to help with houshold chores.

The voyage to the New World was miserable. Adults were allotted a space on the ship about 2 feet (0.6 m) wide and 6 feet (1.8 m) long. Disease spread quickly in the close living quarters. Food was often full of bugs and worms. Many people died.

Once the ships landed in Virginia, colonists who needed servants went aboard and picked out the ones they wanted. After buying the servants' contracts from the ship's captain, the colonists took their new servants home. In Virginia, people called soul-drivers would sometimes buy several servants at one time and *"drive them through the Country like a parcell of Sheep untill they can sell them to advantage."*

Because of a labor shortage in the early 1600s, indentured servants were sometimes forced to work for longer periods than their contracts stated. Servants who tried to run away were punished, and their terms were extended. Only about half of the servants who traveled to Virginia in the 17th century lived to see the end of their contracts.

Not all of the indentured servants in Virginia during the 1600s were white. In the 17th century, most blacks in Virginia were indentured servants. After they completed their contracts, they were free to build their own lives. Some went on to own land, homes, and servants of their own. Not all aspects of life were fair for black servants, however. While white runaway servants generally had their servitude extended by several years, black runaway servants were often sentenced to a lifetime of slavery.

Servants who survived until the end of their contracts received the clothing, tools, and the other items that made up their freedom dues. The lucky ones who were given land were able to achieve a measure of independence. Others worked as tenant farmers or laborers after their terms of indenture were up.

From Servants to Slaves

By the middle of the 17th century, the shift to slavery had begun. Virginia made slavery legal in 1662. In 1705, Virginia's General Assembly passed laws enslaving Africans for life and making the children of black mothers slaves, as well. (Mixed-race children whose mothers were white were indentured for 20 to 30 years.)

Most of the African slaves who arrived in Virginia and other colonies were originally from West and Central Africa. The African slave trade had expanded when Islam spread through northern and western Africa in the 7th century. Arab and African slave traders purchased men, women, and children captured during wars or raids and sold them in slave markets.

Hundreds of slaves are herded toward the British slave ship *Brookes* while some slave traders deal with Africans trying to escape.

When Europeans arrived in West Africa in the mid-1400s, they began trading guns and ammunition for slaves. As Spain expanded its colonies in the Caribbean and the Americas, the demand for slaves in the New World grew. By the time Virginia had embraced the idea of slavery, tens of thousands of Africans were being forced aboard European slave ships each year.

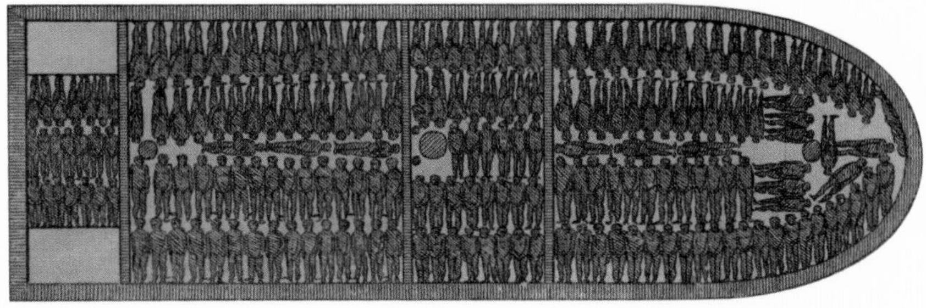

A diagram of the British slave ship *Brookes* illustrates how slaves were packed into cramped, filthy quarters for their passage to the New World.

The sea voyage, known as the Middle Passage, lasted up to two months. The slaves suffered greatly during the voyage. The men were handcuffed together at the wrist and wore leg irons. They slept crowded together below deck, *"so close, as to admit of no other posture than lying on their sides."* The cramped quarters had little fresh air, and diseases spread rapidly. Women were crowded into separate quarters below deck, although they were rarely handcuffed.

During the day, groups of 50 to 60 slaves were brought up and chained to the deck so they could have fresh air. Sailors forced small groups to dance for exercise. Those who refused were whipped. Not surprisingly, many of the slaves died before reaching North America.

Slave Life on the Plantation

The growth of the slave population in Virginia occurred along with the development of the grand plantations in the

18th century. These plantations had thousands of acres planted with tobacco. Slaves planted, weeded, and harvested tobacco from sunup to sundown. It was exhausting work with few breaks.

Not all slaves were agricultural workers. On the largest plantations, male slaves worked as blacksmiths, coopers, brickmakers, carpenters, weavers, and shoemakers, among other jobs. They tended the livestock and drove the carriages. Female slaves cooked and served the meals, made candles and soap, cleaned their owners' houses, and did the laundry.

Even the slave children worked. They helped tend the vegetable gardens and orchards. They milked the cows and gathered eggs. Sometimes, children learned trades such as blacksmithing from other slaves on the plantation.

Most slave quarters were situated so they couldn't be seen from the owner's house. They were usually built near the fields. Each small wooden house had a fireplace, a dirt floor, and a few small windows for fresh air. Several slaves slept in each house.

Most slaves were given a small garden plot near their quarters in order to raise their own fresh vegetables. In addition, they were given weekly rations of food. A typical week's portion for one adult slave was probably 1 peck, or 8 quarts (7.6 l), of cornmeal, 1 pound (0.45 kg) of salt beef, fish, or pork, and possibly some molasses.

Harsh Punishments

Slave owners hired overseers to supervise the slaves. Overseers were unrelenting, forcing slaves to work long hours in inhumane conditions. The overseers often resorted to physical punishment. Whippings were common for both men and women. Some slaves were beaten to death. According to Virginia law, owners who killed their slaves were not guilty of a crime. Owners sometimes ordered overseers to cut off the toes of slaves who had tried to escape. They also might cut off the ear of a slave who lied.

Visitors from England and the northern colonies were often appalled at the treatment of slaves. After traveling through Virginia, Andrew Burnaby of England noted, *"[The gentry's] ignorance of mankind and of learning, exposes them to*

NEW *Discoveries*

Recently, archaeologists working at Thomas Jefferson's Monticello and other plantations in Virginia have discovered pits that were dug into the floors of quarters used by house slaves. Several objects that have been found in these pits provide a glimpse into the slaves' lives. For instance, beads similar to those made in West Africa indicate that people clung to familiar objects in a new and often terrifying world. Gun parts and bones from game animals hint that some slaves may have been allowed to hunt for part of their food.

many errors and prejudices, especially in regard to Indians and Negroes, whom they scarcely consider as of the human species."

Slavery and Freedom

Many of the men from Virginia who spoke out for liberty and the right of Americans to be free were slave owners. Even George Washington, the first President of the United States, owned slaves, although he spoke out against slavery. Virginia's economy had become so dependent upon slavery that no one could figure out how to end it without causing huge financial losses.

Thomas Jefferson, the author of the Declaration of Independence and the third President of the United States, was also a slave owner.

Thomas Jefferson also owned slaves. Jefferson served as the third President of the United States and nearly doubled the size of the country with the Louisiana Purchase. He supported the cause of free public education for all. He founded the University of Virginia. Jefferson shaped the foundation of our country and set a lofty goal for its existence by writing these words in the Declaration of Independence: "*We hold these truths to be self-evident, that all men are created equal.*" How could he believe this and still own slaves?

No easy answer exists. Many of Jefferson's writings indicate that he hated the institution of slavery. He also introduced legislation in Virginia to allow owners to free their slaves. However, when the law passed, Jefferson did not take advantage of it. Of the approximately 600 slaves that Jefferson owned over his lifetime, he freed seven. There is now evidence to suggest that two of these were sons that Jefferson fathered with his slave Sally Hemings after his wife died.

Some people speculate that Jefferson didn't want to damage his political career by acting on the beliefs that appeared in his writings. Others point out that Jefferson was deeply in debt after retiring from the presidency. Perhaps he couldn't afford to give up the slaves that ran his plantation. In any case, in his 1784 book, *Notes on the State of Virginia,* Jefferson referred to slavery as a "*great political and moral evil.*" He also wrote in the book, "*I tremble for my country when I reflect that God is just, that his justice cannot sleep forever.... Nothing is more certainly written in the book of fate than that these people [slaves] are to be free.*" ✻

Demands for Independence

VIRGINIA LEADS THE WAY *as the Colonies move toward independence from Britain.*

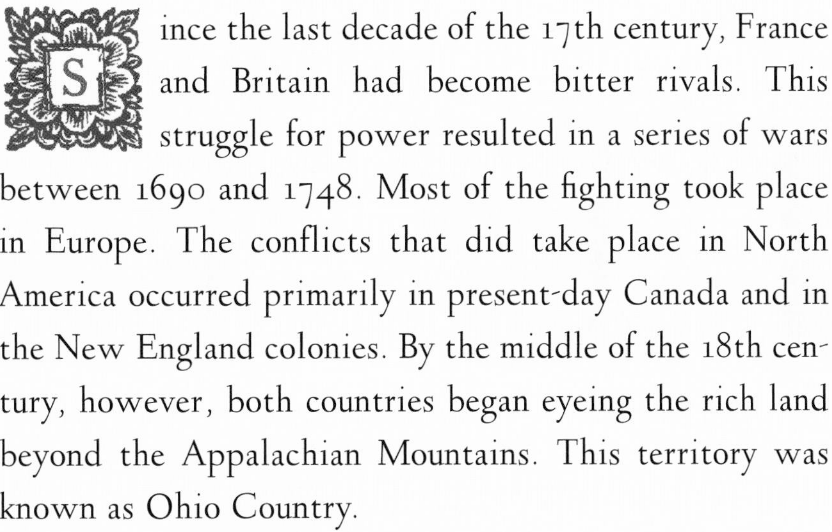

Since the last decade of the 17th century, France and Britain had become bitter rivals. This struggle for power resulted in a series of wars between 1690 and 1748. Most of the fighting took place in Europe. The conflicts that did take place in North America occurred primarily in present-day Canada and in the New England colonies. By the middle of the 18th century, however, both countries began eyeing the rich land beyond the Appalachian Mountains. This territory was known as Ohio Country.

OPPOSITE: George Washington, shown here on horseback, captained the Virginia militia during the French and Indian War. He was just 21 years old.

In 1749, the British government claimed this rich territory. The French, who had sent fur traders into the region for years, believed that the land was rightfully theirs. To strengthen their claim, they began to build forts in northern Ohio Country. Virginia's governor, Robert Dinwiddie, sent 21-year-old Major George Washington, who would one day be the first President of the United States, to order the French out of the territory.

France refused to give up the land and continued to build forts. In 1754, Washington—now a lieutenant colonel—returned with a small company and attacked a French camp. When a large French force struck back, Washington's men had to surrender, and France strengthened its control over all the land west of the Allegheny Mountains. As a result, Great Britain sent troops to the Colonies. The British soldiers built new forts and launched new attacks against the French. The French and Indian War (1754–1763) had begun.

For nine years, British and colonial forces fought against the French and their Indian allies. No battles were fought in present-day Virginia, but many Virginians fought with the British troops. Among them was Washington, who gained a reputation for courage and leadership.

In 1763, the war finally ended in a French defeat. Britain now controlled North America from present-day Canada to Spanish Florida and from the Atlantic Ocean to the Mississippi River. The long war drained the British treasury, and British debts had doubled.

New Restrictions

Though the French and Indian War was over, Native Americans continued to oppose the British. Pontiac's Rebellion in 1763 united Indian nations of the upper Ohio Valley and Great Lakes against the colonists. To avoid being drawn into another costly war, British officials created a western boundary for all the Colonies. Colonial governors from New England to Georgia were forbidden to make any land grants west of this boundary, which became known as the Proclamation Line (*see map page* 67). In Virginia, the Proclamation Line ran parallel to the Blue Ridge mountains. An added benefit was that the boundary line kept the colonists close to the Atlantic coast, where they were easier for the government to control.

The restrictions created by the new boundary threatened the plans of many Virginia land speculators, including Thomas Jefferson, George Washington, George Mason, and Patrick Henry. Either on their own or as partners in land companies, the gentry had been busy obtaining grants to millions of acres beyond the Appalachian Mountains. Unless the boundary was eliminated, the speculators would lose large sums of money. Efforts to reverse the king's decision were unsuccessful.

The Proclamation Line stopped the speculators, but the stream of individual settlers who were looking for land continued to cross the mountains and settle in the Ohio

Growing Resentment

Since its beginning in 1619, the House of Burgesses had been composed of members of the gentry. Early burgesses often passed laws to benefit themselves and other wealthy citizens. By the 18th century, however, debates and discussions more frequently centered on how to strengthen Virginia's whole economy and protect the rights of all Virginians.

In 1740, the House of Burgesses asked the king to withdraw the Navigation Acts. The king denied the request, as well as other requests for control over local matters. By the mid-1700s, Virginians had begun to openly criticize British policies. George Washington and other burgesses deeply resented the fact that the king and Parliament would not give Virginians the same rights as English citizens.

Valley. One contributor to the *Virginia Gazette* noted that *"not even a second Chinese wall, unless guarded by a million of soldiers, could prevent the settlement of the lands on* Ohio [River] *and its dependencies."*

The Stamp Act

In the years following the French and Indian War, the British government looked for ways to pay off its lingering debt. In 1765, Parliament passed the Stamp Act. The Stamp Act required colonial businesses to purchase stamps from the British government to place on all printed materials, such as newspapers, playing cards, and court documents.

In Virginia, long-suppressed resentment over the Navigation Acts boiled over into loud protests against the Stamp Act. In the eyes of Virginians, they had already been paying a heavy price in lost profits for nearly a century due to Britain's trade restrictions. George Washington told a friend that Parliament *"hath no more right to put their hands into my pocket, without my consent, than I have to put my hands into yours for money."*

Colonists were extremely angered by Great Britain's passage of the Stamp Act. This 1765 engraving by John Trumbull shows Virginians stringing up and preparing to tar and feather representatives of the royal government acting as stamp tax collectors.

Patrick Henry, a member of the House of Burgesses, introduced seven resolutions criticizing the Stamp Act. The House of Burgesses passed four of Henry's resolutions. These stated that colonists had the same rights as any other British citizens, including the right to be taxed only by their representatives.

The colonists started a boycott of British goods. Riots broke out in several colonies. In 1766, Parliament finally repealed the act. However, in 1767, Parliament passed the Townshend Acts. These laws placed taxes on British goods such as tea, paint, and lead.

boycott—an agreement made by a group of people to refuse to purchase goods from a nation or company

repeal—to withdraw a law

Colonists once again boycotted British goods, so merchants asked Parliament to repeal the taxes. In 1770, Parliament removed the taxes on all items except tea.

A Threat to Safety

With the population of slaves nearly as high as that of free Virginians, slave owners constantly worried about a widespread revolt. In 1772, the burgesses voted to abolish the Atlantic slave trade. They said this would help prevent "*a Calamity of a most alarming Nature*" that would "*endanger the very Existance of your Majesty's American Dominions.*" Britain, however, refused to stop the slave trade. Declaring independence from Britain seemed to be the only way that Virginians would be able to protect their families from this threat.

The Boston Tea Party

In 1773, Parliament passed the Tea Act which placed a tax on British tea. Parliament believed that colonists would be tempted to buy British tea, which, even though it was taxed, cost less than tea sold by colonial merchants. If the colonists bought the cheaper tea, they would be admitting that Parliament had the right to tax them.

On the evening of December 16, a group of Patriots dressed as Indians crept aboard three ships in Boston Harbor. They dumped 342 boxes of tea into the harbor. This rebellious act became known as the Boston Tea Party.

Patriot—a colonist who favored independence from England

To punish the colonists, Parliament passed a series of laws that became known in the Colonies as the Intolerable Acts. The first one ordered that Boston Harbor be closed, which meant no goods could get in or out of of the colony.

Several colonies, including Virginia, passed resolutions declaring their support for Massachusetts. Upon hearing of Virginia's resolution, the governor—John Murray, Lord Dunmore—disbanded the House of Burgesses. Undeterred, the members met down the street in Ralegh Tavern. This meeting became known as the First Virginia Convention. During the meeting, the burgesses called for all the Colonies to send representatives to Philadelphia, Pennsylvania, to discuss plans for dealing with Parliament.

LEADING *Burgesses*

THE VIRGINIANS WHO SERVED IN the House of Burgesses in the years leading up to the American Revolution (1775–1783) were among the colony's wealthiest and most prominent citizens. They include George Washington, Thomas Jefferson, and Patrick Henry. Their bold words and actions made them leaders in the Colonies' fight for independence.

Some burgesses, including Benjamin Harrison, were very conservative. They did not want to break with England. Richard Henry Lee and others were radicals. They were the most outspoken about calling for independence. In the middle were the moderates. These were men like Peyton Randolph who were willing to consider the necessity of independence from Britain, but who wanted to make sure all peaceful options had been tried first.

PROFILE

George Washington

George Washington was born in 1732. As a boy, he wanted to join the British Navy, but he ended up becoming a land surveyor. When Washington turned 20, his brother Lawrence died. Washington assumed Lawrence's militia responsibilities. Within the year, he was leading Virginia's militia for the British in early battles of the French and Indian War.

After the war, Washington quickly assumed a leadership role in the House of Burgesses. In 1775, the Continental Congress asked Washington to be the commander of the Continental Army. He led his men through six years of battle.

George Washington sat for this portrait painted by Charles Willson Peale in 1772.

Washington became President of the United States in April 1789. He served two terms before retiring to his plantation, Mount Vernon. Three years later, in 1799, Washington died. At his funeral, fellow Virginian Henry Lee praised Washington as *"first in war, first in peace, and first in the hearts of his countrymen."*

Dunmore's Proclamation

Lord Dunmore was not pleased with the number of Virginians who were joining militias. In November 1775, he announced that any slaves belonging to Patriots could earn their freedom by joining Britain in its effort to crush the colonists' rebellion.

Now, even Tories believed that Dunmore had gone too far. By encouraging slaves to fight against their owners, Dunmore had endangered all their lives. As a result, many colonists who had remained neutral or loyal to the British joined the Patriot cause. Richard Henry Lee, one of the leaders of the revolution in Virginia, observed that *"Lord Dunmores unparalleled conduct in Virginia has, a few Scotch excepted, united every Man in that large Colony."*

Tory—a colonist who remained loyal to England; also known as a Loyalist

The Declaration of Independence

On May 15, 1776, members of the Fifth Virginia Convention met in Williamsburg and decided to authorize Virginia to vote for independence at the Continental Congress. The following month, the Virginia Convention issued a Declaration of Rights, written by George Mason, and became the first of the British colonies to

constitution—the written set of guiding laws and principles for a government, state, or society

A Declaration by the Representatives of the UNITED STATES OF AMERICA, in General Congress assembled.

When in the course of human events it becomes necessary for one people to dissolve the political bands which have connected them with another, and to assume among the powers of the earth the separate and equal station to which the laws of nature & of nature's god entitle them, a decent respect to the opinions of mankind requires that they should declare the causes which impel them to the separation.

We hold these truths to be self-evident; that all men are created equal, that they are endowed by their creator with certain [inherent &] inalienable rights; that among these are life, liberty, & the pursuit of happiness; that to secure these rights, governments are instituted among men, deriving their just powers from the consent of the governed; that whenever any form of government becomes destructive of these ends, it is the right of the people to alter or to abolish it, & to institute new government, laying it's foundation on such principles & organising it's powers in such form, as to them shall seem most likely to effect their safety & happiness. prudence indeed will dictate that governments long established should not be changed for light & transient causes: and accordingly all experience hath shewn that mankind are more disposed to suffer while evils are sufferable, than to right themselves by abolishing the forms to which they are accustomed. but when a long train of abuses & usurpations [begun at a distinguished period, &] pursuing invariably the same object, evinces a design to reduce them under absolute Despotism, it is their right, it is their duty, to throw off such government & to provide new guards for their future security. such has been the patient sufferance of these colonies; & such is now the necessity which constrains them to [expunge] alter their former systems of government. the history of the present King of Great Britain is a history of [unremitting] repeated injuries and usurpations, [among which, appears no solitary fact to contradict the uniform tenor of the rest, but all have] in direct object the establishment of an absolute tyranny over these states. to prove this, let facts be submitted to a candid world, [for the truth of which we pledge a faith yet unsullied by falsehood.]

Dr. Franklin's handwriting

Mr. Adams's handwriting

adopt a constitution. Patrick Henry was elected governor of the newly formed Commonwealth of Virginia.

In June, Richard Henry Lee introduced a resolution to the Continental Congress stating *"that these united colonies are and of right ought to be free and independent States."* A committee was formed to write a declaration of independence from Britain. Another group met to draft an outline, called the Articles of Confederation, showing how the states would share power in a new national government. Thomas Jefferson was appointed to the committee writing the declaration, while Lee headed the confederation committee.

The committee charged with drafting a declaration of independence appointed Jefferson and John Adams, a lawyer from Massachusetts, to write the first draft. Adams in turn encouraged Jefferson to write it. He explained why: *"Reason first, you are a Virginian, and a Virginian ought to appear at the head of this business. Reason second, I am obnoxious, suspected, and unpopular. You are very much otherwise. Reason third, you can write ten times better than I can."* Jefferson agreed to do his best.

On July 2, the Congress received word of the British Army's arrival in New York. Immediately, the Congress voted to declare independence from Britain. It wasn't until two days later, however—on July 4—that the Congress finally voted to adopt the Declaration of Independence. The United States of America was born.

OPPOSITE: The first page of Thomas Jefferson's original rough draft of the Declaration of Independence

The New Nation

The American Revolution lasted eight years. At times, it seemed that the Continental Army was on the verge of collapse. General Philip Schuyler grumbled that the men under his command were *"weak in numbers, dispirited, naked, destitute of provisions, without camp equipage, with little ammunition, and not a single piece of cannon."* Then in 1778, France decided to openly help the Americans. This aid proved to be a turning point in the war.

Finally, in 1781, Washington caught up with General Charles Cornwallis and his troops at Yorktown, Virginia. French and American troops surrounded Yorktown, and Cornwallis surrendered to Washington in what was the last battle of the American Revolution. The colonists had defeated the British. A peace treaty was signed in 1783, marking the official end of the war.

Changes were now ahead for the federal government. The weak central government created by the Articles of Confederation had proved to be ineffective. Therefore, in 1787, a constitutional convention was held in Philadelphia. One of Virginia's delegates, James Madison, presented a plan that favored a strong central government. So much of this plan appeared in the final document that Madison is often called the Father of the Constitution. In June 1788, Virginia became the 10th state to join the United States when it voted to ratify, or approve, the U.S. Constitution.

At the same time, the new state formally recommended that a bill of rights, similar to Virginia's Declaration of Rights, be added to the Constitution. In 1791, 10 amendments to the Constitution were ratified by the states. These amendments, known today as the Bill of Rights, guarantee freedom of speech and freedom of religion, among other individual rights.

Virginia's influence on the development of the United States did not end with the ratification of the Constitution. Four of the first five Presidents—George Washington, Thomas Jefferson, James Madison, and James Monroe—were Virginians. Four more Virginians—William Henry Harrison, John Tyler, Zachary Taylor, and Woodrow Wilson—would later serve as President of the United States.

Trapped between the Continental Army (upper, left) and the French fleet (right), General Cornwallis surrendered his troops to George Washington on October 20, 1781, at Yorktown.

Time Line

1578 Sir Humphrey Gilbert receives a charter to establish an English colony in North America.

1583 After claiming Newfoundland for England, Gilbert is lost at sea on the return voyage.

1584 Sir Walter Ralegh receives a charter to establish a colony and sends an expedition to explore the North American coast for a suitable location. He names the region Virginia.

1585 Ralegh sends the first colonists to America, where they establish Roanoke Colony.

1586 Governor Ralph Lane and the other colonists abandon Roanoke Colony.

1587 John White leads a second group of colonists to Roanoke Colony. The colonists celebrate the birth of Virginia Dare, the first English child born in America.

1590 Supply ships find no trace of the colonists on Roanoke Island. The settlement becomes known as the Lost Colony.

1607 English colonists establish Jamestown, the first permanent English settlement in America.

1609 More than 400 colonists die during the Starving Time in the winter of 1609–1610.

1613 John Rolfe sends the first shipment of Virginia tobacco to England.

1619 Virginia colonists are allowed to own land for the first time. The House of Burgesses, a representative government, is established. A Dutch ship brings the first African slaves to Virginia.

1622 Opechancanough and his warriors massacre 350 colonists.

1624 Virginia becomes a royal colony.

1651 Parliament passes the first Navigation Act.

1676 Bacon's Rebellion protests laws and taxes that favor wealthy landowners.

1716 Governor Alexander Spotswood and the Knights of the Golden Horseshoe explore the Blue Ridge region.

1753 Major George Washington orders the French out of the Ohio Country.

1754 The French and Indian War begins.

1763 The French and Indian War ends after nine years of fighting. Parliament establishes the Proclamation Line as the western boundary for its American colonies.

1765 Parliament passes the Stamp Act, which results in colonists' protests against "taxation without representation."

1766 Parliament repeals the Stamp Act.

1767 Parliament imposes new taxes with the Townshend Acts, sparking more protests.

1770 All Townshend duties are repealed except for the tax on tea.

1773 Virginians express outrage over the British response to the Boston Tea Party.

1774 Virginia sends delegates to the First Continental Congress in Philadelphia.

1775 Patrick Henry delivers his famous "Give me liberty or give me death" speech in Richmond. The Battles of Lexington and Concord launch the American Revolution. George Washington is named commander in chief of the Continental Army.

1776 Virginia delegates along with other representatives at the Second Continental Congress vote to accept the Declaration of Independence.

1781 British general Charles Cornwallis surrenders at Yorktown after the last battle of the American Revolution.

1788 Virginia ratifies the Constitution and becomes the 10th U.S. state.

RESOURCES

BOOKS

*Berlin, Ira. *Generations of Captivity: A History of African American Slaves.* Cambridge, Massachusetts: Belknap Press, 2003.

*Billings, Warren. *Sir William Berkeley and the Forging of Colonial Virginia.* Baton Rouge, Louisiana: Louisiana State University Press, 2004.

Bruchac, Joseph. *Pocahontas.* Orlando, Fla.: Silver Whistle, 2003.

Collier, Christopher, and James Lincoln Collier. *The Paradox of Jamestown.* New York: Benchmark Books, 1998.

Hakim, Joy. *A History of US: Making Thirteen Colonies.* New York: Oxford University Press, 2002.

Hariot, Thomas. *A Briefe and True Report of the New Found Land of Virginia.* New York: Dover Publications, 1972.

King, David C. *Colonies and Revolution.* Hoboken, N.J.: Wiley, 2003.

*Morgan, Philip. *Slave Counterpoint: Black Culture in the Eighteenth-Century Chesapeake and Lowcountry.* Chapel Hill, North Carolina: University of North Carolina Press, 1998.

Masoff, Joy. *Colonial Times 1600–1700.* New York: Scholastic Reference, 2000.

McDaniel, Melissa. *The Powhatan Indians.* New York: Chelsea House, 1996.

*Rhys, Isaac. *The Transformation of Virginia, 1740–1790.* Chapel Hill, North Carolina: University of North Carolina Press, 1982.

** college-level sources*

WEB SITES

Association for the Preservation of Virginia Antiquities (APVA)—Jamestown Rediscovery
http://www.apva.org/jr.html
Information about the Jamestown Rediscovery archaeological project being undertaken by the APVA can be found at this Web site.

Colonial Williamsburg
http://www.history.org
The official Web site of colonial Williamsburg contains information about the people and history of the colony of Virginia.

The Library of Congress Presents America's Story from America's Library
http://www.americaslibrary.gov/cgi-bin/page.cgi
This Web page for kids from the Library of Congress contains fascinating information on Virginia and other American colonies.

Virginia Historical Society—The Story of Virginia: An American Experience
http://www.vahistorical.org/storyofvirginia.htm
This online exhibit of different periods in Virginia's history is presented by the Virginia Historical Society.

Virtual Jamestown
http://www.virtualjamestown.org
This site provides interactive maps and first-hand accounts of the "Virginia experiment."

Quote Sources

CHAPTER ONE

p. 16 "this island had many" and "above a hundreth islands." http://personal.pitnet.net/primarysources/barlowe.html. Hakluyt, Richard. *The Principall Voyages, Traffiques, and Discourses of the English Nations* (1599–1600). Hart, Albert Bushnell, ed. *American History Told by Contemporaries, Volume 1*. New York: 1898, pp. 89–95; p. 18 "very handsome and goodly people" and "we found the people." http://personal.pitnet.net/primarysources/barlowe.html. Hakluyt and Hart; p. 25 "several of their ancestors." http://docsouth.unc.edu/nc/lawson/ lawson.html. Lawson, John. *A New Voyage to Carolina; Containing the Exact Description and Natural History of That Country: Together with the Present State Thereof. And a Journal of a Thousand Miles, Travel'd Thro' Several Nations of Indians. Giving a Particular Account of Their Customs, Manners, &c.* London: 1709.

CHAPTER TWO

p. 32 "upon this plot." http://etext.lib.virginia.edu/etcbin/jamestown-rowse?id=J1002. Percy, George. *Observations gathered out of a Discourse of the Plantation of the Southerne Colonie in Virginia by the English*, 1606; p. 33 "there was no talke." http://memory.loc.gov/cgibin/query/r?ammem/lhbcb:@field(DOCID+@lit(lhbcb0262adiv13)). Smith, John. *The generall historie of Virginia, New England & the Summer Isles, together with The true travels, adventures and observations, and A sea grammar, Volume 1*, Chapter 3, p. 109; p. 37 "[the Powhatan Indians] adorne themselves most." http://etext.lib.virginia.edu/etcbin/jamestown-browse?id=J1008. Smith, John. *A MAP OF VIRGINIA. WITH A DESCRIPTION OF THE COUNTREY, THE Commodities, People, Government and Religion.* Oxford: Joseph Barnes,1612.

CHAPTER THREE

p. 40 "our men were destroyed." http://etext.lib.virginia.edu/etcbin/jamestown-browse?id=J1002. Percy, George. *Observations gathered out of a Discourse of the Plantation of the Southerne Colonie in Virginia by the English*, 1606; p. 41 "two great stones." http://memory.loc.gov /cgibin/query/r?ammem/lhbcb:@field (DOCID+@lit(lhbcb0262adiv13)). Smith, John. *The generall historie of Virginia, New England & the Summer Isles, together with The true travels, adventures and observations, and A sea grammar, Volume 1*, Chapter 3, p. 101; p. 43 "he that will not work." http://www.history.org/foundation/journal/smith.cfm. Montgomery, Dennis. "Captain John Smith." *Colonial Williamsburg Journal*, Volume 16, Number 3, Spring 1994. Williamsburg, VA: © Colonial Williamsburg Foundation, 2005, p. 14; p. 44 "I entreat you." http://www.usconstitution.com/CaptJohnSmithTheGenerallHistorieofVirginia.htm. Smith, John. *The generall historie of Virginia, New England & the Summer Isles, together with The true travels, adventures and observations, and A sea grammar, Volume 1*, Chapter 5; p. 45 "horses and other beastes" and "dogs catts." http://etext.lib.virginia.edu/ etcbin/ jamestown-browse?id=J1063. Percy, George. *A Trewe Relacyon of the Pcedeinges and Ocurrentes of Momente wch have hapned in Virginia from the Tyme Sr Thomas GATES was shippwrackte uppon the BERMUDES ano 1609 untill my depture outt of the Country wch was in ano Dñi 1612.* Tyler, Lyon Gardiner. *Tyler's Quarterly Historical and Genealogical Magazine*, Volume III, Number 4. Richmond, VA: Virginia Historical Pageant, April 1922, p. 267; p. 47 "a custom loathsome." http:// curry.edschool.virginia.edu /socialstudies/projects/jvc/overview.html. King James I. *A Counterblast to Tobacco*. London: R.B., 1604.

CHAPTER FOUR

p. 57 "men of worth" and "at last Christmas." http://etext.lib.virginia.edu/etcbin/jamestown-browse?id=J1080. *A Perfect Description of VIRGINIA*. London: Peter Force, 1837; p. 57 "soe very little." Holton, Woody. *Forced Founders: Indians, Debtors, Slaves, & the Making of the American Revolution in Virginia*. Chapel Hill, NC: University of North Carolina Press, 1999, p. 48. Billings, Warren M., John E. Selby, and Thad W. Tate. *Colonial Virginia: A History*. White Plains, NY: KTO Press, 1986, p. 79; p. 58 "an evil we with patience." Holton, p. 48. "A Virginian." Rind's *Virginia Gazette*, December 11, 1766; p. 59 "all Indians in generall." Morgan, Edmund S. American *Slavery, American Freedom*. New York: W.W. Norton & Co., 1975, p. 255.

CHAPTER FIVE

p. 63 "of about two hundred houses." http://134.76.163.65/agora docs/2332BIBLIOGRAPHIC DESCRIPTION.html. Burnaby, Andrew. *Travels through the middle settlements in North-America, in the years 1759 and 1760; with observations upon the State of the Colonies.* London: T. Payne, 1798, p. 4.

CHAPTER SIX

p. 72 "indolent, easy" and "immoderately fond of dancing." http://134.76.163.65/agora docs/2332BIBLIOGRAPHIC DESCRIPTION.html. Burnaby, Andrew. *Travels through the middle settlements in North-America, in the years 1759 and 1760; with observations upon the State of the Colonies.* London: T. Payne, 1798, p. 18 and p. 21; p. 74 "eight of Mr. Carters sons." http://www.indiana.edu/~jah/teaching/2003 09/. Fithian, Philip Vickers. *Journal*, 1766–1775. Excerpt from November 1, 1773; p. 76 "men are generally." Urmstone, Rev. John. Excerpt from a letter. http://www.full-books.com/American-Negro-Slavery2.html. Hawks, F.L. *History of North Carolina, Volume 2*. Fayetteville, NC, 1857, 1858, pp. 215–216.

CHAPTER SEVEN

p. 81 "drive them through the country." http://historymatters.gmu.edu/d/6624.html. Harrower, John. "Many Hundreds are Sterving for Want of Employment: John Harrower Leaves London for Virginia, 1774." *The Journal of John Harrower, An Indentured Servant in the Colony of Virginia*, 1773–1776. New York: Holt, Rinehart, and Winston, 1963; p. 81 "during the voyage." http://www.ukans.edu/ carrie/docs/texts/gottlieb.html. Mittelberger, Gottlieb. "On the Misfortune of Indentured Servants." Eben, Carl Theo., trans. *Gottlieb Mittelberger's Journey to Pennsylvania in the Year 1750 and Return to Germany in the Year 1754*. Philadelphia: John Jos. McVey, 1898, pp. 19–29; p. 83 "so close, as to admit." http://occawlonline.pearsoned.com/bookbind/pubbooks/divine5e/medialib/timeline/docs/sources/theme primarysources Slavery 7.html. Falconbridge, Alexander. *The African Slave Trade*, 1788; p. 86 "[the gentry's] ignorance." http://134.76.163.65/agora docs/2332BIBLIOGRAPHIC DESCRIPTION.html. Burnaby, Andrew. *Travels through the middle settlements in North-America, in the years 1759 and 1760; with observations upon the State of the Colonies.* London: T. Payne, 1798, p. 18; p. 87 "we hold these truths." http://etext.lib.virginia.edu/etcbin/toccernew2?id=JefVirg.sgm&images=images/modeng&data=/texts/english/modeng/parsed&tag=public&part=all. Jefferson, Thomas. *Notes on the State of Virginia*, 1784 ; p. 87 "great political and moral evil" and "I tremble for my country." http://etext.lib.virginia.edu/etcbin/toccernew2?id=JefVirg.sgm&images=images/modeng&data=/texts/english/modeng/parsed&tag=public&part=all. Jefferson.

CHAPTER EIGHT

p. 92 "not even a second." Holton, Woody. *Forced Founders: Indians, Debtors, Slaves, & the Making of the American Revolution in Virginia*. Chapel Hill, NC: University of North Carolina Press, 1999, p. 7. "A Friend to the True Interest of Britain in America." Rind's *Virginia Gazette*, January 14, 1773; p. 93 "hath no more right." http://www.history.org/Almanack/people/bios/biowash2.cfm. "George Washington." Williamsburg, VA: © Colonial Williamsburg Foundation, 2005; p. 94 "a calamity" and "endanger the very existance." Holton, p. 71. *Revolutionary Virginia: The Road to Independence, Volume 1*. Van Schreeven, William J., Robert L. Scribner, and Brent Tarter, eds. Charlottesville, VA: 1973–1983, pp. 85–88; p. 96 "gentlemen may cry." http://www.history.org/Almanack/ life/politics/giveme.cfm. Henry, Patrick. Speech given at St. John's Church, Richmond, Virginia, March 23, 1775; p. 97 "declare freedom to the slaves." Holton, p. 145. "Deposition of Dr. William Pasteur. In Regard to the Removal of Powder from the Williamsburg Magazine." *Virginia Magazine of History and Biography, Volume 8*, 1905, p. 49; p. 98 "first in war." http://www.cr.nps.gov/ museum/exhibits/revwar/image gal/indeimg/lhenry.html. National Park Service Museum Collections, American Revolutionary War. Portraits from the Southern Theater: Henry Lee; p. 99 "Lord Dunmores unparalleled conduct." Holton, p. 158–159. Lee, Richard Henry, to Catherine Macauley, November 29, 1775. Hoffman, Paul P., ed. *The Lee Family Papers*, 1742–1795. Charlottesville, VA: University of Virginia Library, 1966; p. 101 "that these united colonies." http://www.historicaldocuments.com/LeeResolution.htm. Lee, Richard Henry. Speech made before the Second Continental Congress, June 7, 1776; p. 101 "reason first." http://www.eyewitnesstohistory.com/jefferson.htm. *Writing the Declaration of Independence*, 1776. Eyewitness to History, 1999; p. 102 "weak in numbers." http://encarta.msn.com/. "American Revolution." Microsoft® Encarta® Online Encyclopedia 2005 © Microsoft Corporation, 1997–2005.

INDEX

About the Author and Consultant

SANDY POBST has 20 years experience in the educational field, writing books for middle graders with social studies and science-based content, developing educational software, and writing teacher guides for use in the classroom. A former elementary school teacher, Pobst's latest projects include a series of books on immigrants in America and cultures of the Middle East. She holds a Bachelor of Science degree in Elementary Education from Kansas State University. She lives with her husband and two children in Austin, Texas.

KEVIN D. ROBERTS is an assistant professor of history at New Mexico State University. He earned his Ph.D. in colonial American history at the University of Texas at Austin, and his M.A. from Virginia Tech, where his thesis examined African-American culture and family networks in colonial and antebellum Virginia. He has published numerous articles and chapters on various aspects of slavery and race in the old South. His ancestors hail from one of the original Cajun families of southern Louisiana.

Illustration Credits

Cover, title page,
pages 33, 38, 82, 83:
Picture Collection, The Branch Libraries, The New York Public Library

Pages 9, 12, 17, 26, 34, 42, 47, 50, 53, 62, 68, 80, 86, 88, 93, 98:
The Granger Collection

Pages 11, 75:
American Antiquarian Society

Pages 18, 21, 36:
Bridgeman Art Library

Page 22:
© The Mariners' Museum/CORBIS

Pages 29, 67:
© National Geographic Society

Pages 48, 54:
Art Resources

Pages 56, 64, 70, 72, 73:
Colonial Williamsburg Foundation

Pages 60, 78:
© Bettmann/CORBIS
Page 103:
© CORBIS

End sheets, 8, 100:
The Library of Congress

NORTH AMERICA Divided into its III PRINCIPALL PARTS 1st ENGLISH Part Viz ENGLISH EMPIRE
N Foundland N Scotland N England N York N Jarsey Pensylvania Maryland Virginia Carolina Carolania or Florida California Sommer I's Bahama I's Jamaica
1685
NEW NORTH WALES
NEW SOUTH WALES
Tract of Land full of Wild Bulls
NEW MEXICO
NEW MEXICO
NEW ALBION
CALIFORNIA
SEA OF CALIFORNIA
NEW BISCAIA
ZACATECAS
LAKE SUPERIOR
THE GOLF OR BAY OF MEXICO
SEA OF NEW SPAIN
YUCATAN
HONDURAS